A PEOPLE'S ECOLOGY

A PEOPLE'S ECOLOGY
Explorations in Sustainable Living

EDITED BY
Gregory Cajete

CLEAR LIGHT PUBLISHERS
SANTA FE, NEW MEXICO

Copyright © 1999 Gregory Cajete
Clear Light Publishers, 823 Don Diego, Santa Fe, NM 87501
WEB: www.clearlightbooks.com

First Edition
10 9 8 7 6 5 4 3 2 1

Library of Congress Cataloging-in-Publication Data

Cajete, Gregory, ed.
A people's ecology : explorations in sustainable living : health,
environment, agriculture, native traditions / Gregory Cajete.
      p.   cm.
   Includes bibliographical references (p.   ) and index.
   ISBN: 1-57416-028-1
      1. Pueblo Indians—Food. 2. Pueblo Indians—Nutrition.
3. Pueblo Indians—Agriculture. 4. Human ecology—Southwest, New. 5. Food habits—Southwest, New. 6. Sustainable
agriculture—Southwest, New. 7. Sustainable development—
Southwest, New. I. Cajete, Gregory, 1952–   .
   E99.P9P39   1999
   363.8'08997—dc21   99-24062
                                                              CIP

Cover Design: Carol O'Shea
Interior Design/Typography: Vicki S. Elliott
Cover Photo © Ronnie Kaufman, Stock Market
Back Cover Photo and Frontispiece © Marcia Keegan

Contents

Introduction

Gregory Cajete

A People's Ecology is a unique contribution toward a more complete understanding of the nature of health, ecology, and sustainable living among diverse peoples. The collection is focused on the interrelated themes of cultural identity, health, relationship to the environment, environmental restoration, and organic foods as part of a greater whole. As such, the various "stories" in the collection provide a strategic basis for understanding how sustainable living can be achieved and maintained.

Several contributors mention the state of health among Native Americans and other Indigenous populations with similar histories of oppression, and similar current struggles with environmental, health, and sustainable living issues. Environmental degradation resulting from pollution, poverty, and bio-social epidemiology such as diabetes, alcoholism, physical abuse, and high rates of suicide are all related symptoms of "ethno-stress" caused by the disruption of culture and loss of land base among Indigenous peoples.

Some contributors are candid in their assertions that the modern mind-set must integrate understanding of Indigenous peoples' traditional relationship with the land in order to achieve long-term sustainability, not only for Native communities, but for everyone everywhere. Implied here is the essence of the conflict between world views: nonanthropocentric (Indigenous) versus anthropocentric (Western industrial). The former is grounded on the interconnectedness of humans with the land and natural forces in general, as well as with all other living creatures. In contrast, the latter tends to separate living creatures and nonorganic matter into hierarchies with humans at the center or pinnacle of all.

This collection essentially describes an underlying ecology of health and sustainability in terms of the ways that it was historically expressed, its current state of disruption, and possibilities for a more ideal and revitalized future. The contributors challenge us to reclaim our collective heritage of caring for our "home fires," a metaphor for the traditional Indigenous sense for and understanding of connections among people, animals, plants, and natural forces. In this way the book honors the paradigm of an Indigenous understanding of sustainability, succinctly stated in the phrase "healthy environment, healthy culture, healthy people." It is this paradigm that the contributors view as paramount and around which they weave the various and complex issues of community, cultural awareness, environmental health, and ecological theory as they apply to the practice of health care, agriculture, architecture, environmental justice, and social activism. In doing this, *A People's Ecology* opens new avenues of dialogue for re-energizing awareness, creating educational curricula, and initiating social change.

The book begins with an exploration of orientation to place, which then leads to exploring understandings of sources of life, health and healing, and reflections on diet, agriculture, building, and marketing organic products. Each of the contributing authors advocates a closer look at the environmental wisdom that has inherently guided Indigenous and relatively recent alternative lifestyles. This inherent wisdom continues to be ignored for the most part by mainstream education and media as areas for serious discussion and research. In addition, each author illustrates the application of a sustainable living model for educating the public as a way of teaching about more than just immediate environmental concerns to include the broader physical, social, cultural, and political elements related to holistic health and people's long-term welfare.

In the first chapter, "Look to the Mountain," I talk about the Indigenous sense of connection to one's land and how that sense of connection gives rise to expressions in dance, ritual, art, agriculture, and community life. This model of an ancient tradition of obligation, responsibility, and mutual reciprocity forms the backdrop for the discussions of food, agriculture, health, housing, and sustainability which follow.

In "Nourishing Gifts," Brett Bakker discusses the ancient and recent origins of traditional foods of the Pueblo culture, what makes a food "traditional," and how changes in diet and lifestyle have impacted on the Pueblo peoples' present and future. The message of Bakker's piece segues into Kenny Ausubel's essay, " 'It Is Time to Plant': The Real Green Revolution," a description of efforts to collect and preserve biodiversity in the form of food and medicinal plant seeds. These programs are aimed at providing for and supplementing alternative ways of farming.

Next in the lineup is my essay titled "Indigenous Foods, Indigenous Health: A Pueblo Perspective," an historical overview of Pueblos' relationship with the land, animals, and plants from ancient times to the present. I relate how understanding this history is important to the continued health of the Pueblo peoples.

Enrique Salmón is an ethnobotanist of Rarámuri (Tarahumara Indian) ancestry. In "Traditional Diet and Health in Northwestern Mexico," he portrays a traditional Rarámuri culture which continues to rely upon a diet of traditional foods and as a result suffers from significantly fewer nutritionally related diseases. The Rarámuri continue their food traditions because a "Big Gulp culture" has not yet emerged in Rarámuri country due to the lack of supermarkets, convenience stores, and fast food restaurants. Yet all these things will come to Rarámuri country in time.

In "A Navajo Meditates on Food and Culture," Lawrence Shorty, a Navajo health educator, creates a context for understanding the deeper nature of sustainability as expressed in the food that people choose to eat. As his grandfather surmises, "when we eat other people's food, we begin to think and become like them." This statement reflects the crux of the plight of Indigenous peoples as they attempt to adapt themselves to a world that is not of their making, with dire effects such as heart disease, diabetes, and alcoholism.

Clayton Brascoupe, a Mohawk of the Iroquois Six Nations, describes his life and work in "Reflections of a Native American Farmer." He raises organic foods and uses traditional Native American methods whenever possible on his farm at the Tesuque Pueblo in northern New Mexico.

In "Daybreak Farm and Food Project Seeks Revitalization of White Corn Usage," John Mohawk and Yvonne Dion-Buffalo describe a program dedicated to helping farmers of the Iroquois Six Nations grow and market white corn. The Daybreak Project is an outcome of the understanding of the interrelatedness of culture, agricultural practices, food preferences, diet, and the overall health of a people.

Eliseo Torres describes common physical, mental, and spiritual conditions and treatments in "Rituals and Practices of Folk Healers in the U.S. Southwest and Mexico." In "Curanderismo as Holistic Medicine," Gilbert Arizaga elaborates on *curanderismo* as a healing system, in which the patient must participate in healing along with family and (often) community members.

In "Permaculture as a Way of Seeing and Acting in the World," Joel Glanzberg outlines the philosophy and principles of permaculture as a way to introduce a practiced understanding of how the planet we live on really works, and a recognition of our ultimate interdependence therein. Glanzberg focuses on the principle of "all things garden," based on the essential natural reality of life, the continual interaction of plants, animals, and earth at all levels of ecology. He talks about permaculture theory which parallels the Indigenous view of interactive relationship and interdependence, and demonstrates how contemporary permaculture parallels traditional Native American views of relationship and "natural democracy" or the inherent right of all living things to exist.

In "Renaissance of Ancient Building Practices," architect Paula Baker explains the need for using locally available building materials as an effective way to enhance the health of the environment and of the human beings who live and work in buildings of all kinds. In outlining the principles of baubiology—the study of how buildings affect human health—Baker discusses the use of environmentally benign building materials and siting and designing structures according to ancient understandings of the planet's electromagnetic fields and the architectural proportion and harmonic order of space.

John Macker emphasizes the importance of including a broad and comprehensive view of the organic foods market in the education of the public about the food they buy. For John the question is not that consumer education should include environmental awareness, health, diet, nutrition, and living on the Earth, but how it should be included. John believes that all businesses must integrate an awareness of responsibility for care of the environment as a necessary part of serving their clients. Food quality, environmental toxicity, and degradation affect all, and must be taken seriously as factors in the training and continued professional practice of all food-related businesses.

In the final analysis, *A People's Ecology* is a vision of what can be if health care advocates, educators, and ecologically motivated practitioners in all professions open themselves to the creative possibilities inherent in the Indigenous metaphor, "healthy environment, healthy culture, healthy people." May the good spirits guide and keep you as you read *A People's Ecology,* for you too are called upon to be a keeper of sustainable living. *Be With Life!*

1

"Look to the Mountain" Reflections on Indigenous Ecology

Gregory Cajete

Corn field on Hopi land in Arizona. Photograph © Marcia Keegan.

The Americas are an ensouled and enchanted geography, and the relationship of Indian people to this geography embodies a "theology of place," reflecting the very essence of what may be called spiritual ecology. American Indians' traditional relationship to and participation with the landscape includes not only the land itself but the way in which they have perceived themselves and all else. Through generations of living in America, Indian people have formed and been formed by the land. Indian kinship with the land, its climate, soil, water, mountains, lakes, forests, streams, plants, and animals has literally determined the expressions of an American Indian theology. The land has become an extension of Indian thought and being because, in the words of a Pueblo elder, "It is this place that holds our memories and the bones of our people...This is the place that made us."

There is a metaphor that Pueblo people use, which, when translated into English, means "that place that the People talk about." This metaphor refers not only to a physical place but also a place of consciousness and an orientation to sacred ecology. Sacred orientation to place and space is a key element of the ecological awareness and intimate relationship that Indians have established with the North American landscape for 30,000 years or more. Indian people have names for all places that comprise important environmental features of the landscape. In fact, Indian languages are replete with environmentally derived references based on the kind of natural characteristics and experiences they have had living in relationship with their respective landscapes.

Another metaphor used by Tewa elders is *pin peye obe* (look to the mountain), which is used to remind people of the long view, or the need to think about what we are doing in terms of its impact on future generations. "Look to the mountain" reminds us that when dealing with the landscape we must think in terms of many thousands of years.

Theology of Place

In the words of an Acoma Pueblo poet, the place "that Indian people talk about" is not only a physical place with sun, wind, rain, water, lakes, rivers, and streams, but a spiritual place, a place of being and understanding. Sense of place is constantly evolving and transforming through the lives and relationships of all participants. Humans naturally have a geographic sensibility and geographic imagination borne of millions of years of interaction with places. Humans have always oriented themselves by establishing direct and personal relationships to places in the landscapes with which they have interacted.

An ecological sense of relationship encompassed every aspect of traditional American Indian life. American Indians understood that an intimate relationship between themselves and their environment was the essence of their survival and identity as people. Native peoples lived in every place in what Europeans called the New World, and in every place they established a direct and enduring relationship with the natural environment. They transmitted this understanding of relationship in every aspect of their lives—language, art, music, dance, social organization, ceremony, and identity as human beings.

Adaptations to place among Indigenous groups in America took many forms. Living in the forests of the Northeast, Indians venerated the trees and integrated that reality of their environment into every aspect of their lives and expression as a people. Living on the Plains, Indians followed the buffalo and made themselves portable in the way of all nomadic hunters around the world. They understood and expressed themselves in relationship to the land and the animals upon which they depended for their survival. In the desert Southwest, Pueblo Indians became dryland farmers and likewise venerated the cycles of water, earth, wind, and fire—all environmental elements essential to life and to the continuance of the Pueblo people in their place. The fisher and forest people in the Pacific Northwest established intimate relationships with the salmon upon which they depended for life, with the sea mammals they encountered, and the great rain forests that characterized the environment of their place. And in similar fashion, relationships to place were established by all other peoples such as the Paiute in the Great Basin, the Seminole in the Everglades, and the various Eskimo groups throughout the Far North.

Tribes adapted to specific environments in unique and different ways, which in turn gave rise to a diversity of expressive cultures. However, although Native peoples' cultures were quite diverse, there was also adherence to a common set of life principles. They understood that the natural universe was imbued with life and sacredness. They understood that their effects on their place had to be carried out with humility, understanding, and respect for the sacredness of the place and all living things of those places. They expressed a "theology of place," which, while focused specifically on their place, extended to include all of nature. The environments of diverse

Indian peoples may have been different, but the basis of their theology was the same. The very word "indigenous" is derived from the Latin root *indu* or *endo,* which in turn is related to the Greek word *endina,* which means "entrails." "Indigenous" means being so completely identified with a place that you reflect its very entrails, its insides, its soul.

For Native people throughout the Americas, the paradigm of thinking, acting, and working evolved because of and through their established relationships to nature. As such, the foundation, expression, and context of Indigenous education was environmental. The theology of nature reverberated throughout art, community, myth, and any other aspect of human social or tribal expression. All were inspired and formed through an integrated and direct relationship of making a living in and through the reality of their physical environments.

The environment was not separate or divorced from Native peoples' lives, but rather was the context or set of relationships that tied everything together. They understood ecology not as something apart from themselves or outside their intellectual reality, but rather as the very center and generator of self-understanding. As a center, that environmental understanding became the guiding mechanism for the ways in which they expressed themselves and their sense of sacredness.

Windows into Natural Affiliation

Sacred orientation to place is a key concept in Indigenous education. Indigenous peoples honored their place, and often considered themselves to be situated in the center of a sacred space that had very distinct orientations. They recognized and named their directional relationships in terms of the natural and relational qualities associated with them. For instance, many American Indian tribes named the cardinal directions in a way that included a description of the way people oriented themselves upon facing the sun. Thus, north may be referred to as "to the left side of the sun rising"; south, "to the right side of the sun rising"; east, "to the sun rising"; and west, "to the sun setting."

This is the way Indigenous people metaphorically represent the physical qualities of directionality in their language. Such qualities would be included with others, including colors, plants, animals, winds, kinds of thought, and features of the landscape of place that they associated with each direction. Orientation is essential for Indigenous people because each person belongs to a place. Understanding orientation to place is essential in order to grasp what it means to be related. Many Indigenous peoples recognize seven directions: the four cardinal directions, above, center, and below. This way of viewing orientation creates a (literal) sphere of relationship founded on place that evolves through time and space.

Art is another reflection of Indigenous relational sensibility and education. For example, the design motifs of such ancient Southwestern Mimbres pottery reflect the integration of humans with animals, and the relationship the Mimbres felt with animals, plants, and nature in general. Primal symbols of nature also abound in contemporary Pueblo art forms that represent key features, elements, or foundations of their ecological relationships. One is the Pueblo cloud motif. This important symbol reflects the importance of water, the nature of water to flow in various states and cycles, and the ecological understanding of how water circulates in a semi-arid environment. Pueblo elders recognized many different kinds of rain.

They understood that in their arid environment, rain was essential to the life cycle, and therefore their own survival. The elders watched clouds day in and day out. Centuries of such observations permitted them to discern the relationships and characteristics of clouds. They reflected on how water is intimately involved with the nature of clouds. They recognized all types of rain that would be possible from particular kinds of clouds. And they prayed for the kinds of clouds that brought the qualities of water they needed. Whether snow, sleet, wind with rain, baby rain, grandfather rain, or mother rain, they honored the kinds of rain that brought them life.

Relationship with Animals

Hunting and planting are two strains of mythic tribal expression. In many cultures, such as the Pueblo, both orientations are represented in the evolution of traditional art designs, mythic themes, dance, and ritual. The understanding gained from animals about ecological transformation was portrayed in many forms, and wherever Indian people hunted, these traditions abounded. Once again, while each tribe reflected these understandings in unique ways, core understandings were similar from tribe to tribe. The essential focus was relationship, and the guiding sentiment was respect. The central intent revolved around honoring the entities that gave life to a people. Whether it was hunting in the Southwest or in the Far North, an intimate relationship between the hunter and the hunted was established. There was an ecological understanding that animals transformed themselves, and that while this may not be a literal transformation, indeed it is an ecological reality. Animals eat other animals, and the animals that are eaten become a part of the substance of other life. This is the primary process of transformation of energy in the animal kingdom. Through observation and interaction with animals over generations, Indigenous people understood that animals could teach people something about the essence of transformation. Indigenous peoples have created many kinds of symbolic ideals in reflections about themselves and their relationship to animals. The essence of one such ideal is captured in the metaphoric construct of the "hunter of good heart." Hunting in and of itself is both a spiritual and educational act. Hunting is one of those 40,000-year courses of study that human beings have been involved with. The hunter of good heart was a bringer of life to his people: he had to have not only a very intimate knowledge of the animals he hunted, but also a deep and abiding respect for their nature, procreation, and continuance as species. While he tracked the animal physically to feed himself and his family, he also tracked the animal ritually, thereby understanding at a deeper level his relationship with the animals he hunted. The hunted animal became one of the guides of relationship and community in Indigenous education.

In the entire process of Indigenous hunting, there was always a time for teaching. That time was often directly expressed when the hunter brought back his catch. A scene in many traditional American Indian and Alaska Native communities is when a hunter returns from the hunt, says prayers of thanksgiving to the animals he has killed, and then gathers his extended family around him. He then tells the story of the animal that has been slain. He talks about the importance of maintaining the proper relationship to the animal that has given its life to perpetuate the life of his family and community. He expresses to his family why it is so important to continue to understand that life is sacred, and that animal life also begets human life through the sacrifice of its flesh to feed and clothe humans. He reminds all that human beings will provide the repayment of life through their own flesh for the purpose of perpetuating animal life. The necessity of sharing is also symbolically emphasized through the hunter sharing his catch with his extended family. These symbolic acts of respect and remembrance reinforce communal relationship to the animals that gave their lives for a community's benefit. Teaching by the hunter of good heart is a way of remembering to remember relationship.

The myths of Indigenous people in North America are replete with animal characters that embody the people's understanding of what it means to live in reverent relationship with animals and the natural world. Each story is a complex of metaphors that teach the essential importance of proper relationship and respect for the natural world. Each illustrates the fact that all living things and natural entities have a role to play in maintaining the web of life.

The Iroquois relate a myth in which Opossum, who was very conceited about his elegant and busy tail, was tricked by Cricket and Hare into shaving his tail. Opossum believed his tail would become even more glorious upon shaving it, but of course, he failed. This tale is a reflection on how people can get carried away by egotistical desires.

The Paiutes relate a tale that describes the stealing of fire by Coyote after he challenged powerful shamans who lived on an obsidian mountain. The shamans had captured the fire, and refused to share it with the animals or the rest of the world. So the world remained in cold and darkness. Coyote and other animals challenged the shamans to a dance contest. Coyote and the shamans dance until all except Coyote fall asleep from exhaustion. Coyote then steals the last embers of the dance fire and runs away with the shamans in hot pursuit. As Coyote and the other animals and birds take turns running with the fire throughout the land, they shed light and warmth upon the dark frozen landscape.

There are other myths about human relationships to animals, such as the well-known Northwest Indian myth about the woman who married a bear. The relationships of bears and the similarities of bears to human beings underlie the importance American Indian people place on treating bears respectfully. The role of birds such as Raven in the creation of the first man and first woman is related in a myth from the Eskimo, which tells of the creation of the first human from a pea pod.

Another way of remembering to remember relationship is the complex of animal dances found among Indigenous people around the world. Animal dances are a commemoration of humans' continued relationship with the animal world. The purpose of Indigenous dances is not only the renewal of opportunities for remembering to remember. They also help to maintain the balance of all essential relationships of the world. Such is the case with the Yurok White Deerskin Dance, which was performed to ensure the balance of the world from one year to the next. Indigenous people felt responsibility not only for themselves, but also for the entire world around them. The world renewal ceremonies conducted by all Indigenous people are reflections of this deep ecological sensibility and responsibility.

Indigenous people created annual ceremonial cycles based on the belief that acknowledgment of the sources of a community's life must be made year in and year out. Ceremonial cycles are based on the understanding that people have to continue to remember and perpetuate essential ecological relationships through the lives of individual tribal members and succeeding generations. Once people break the cycles of remembering they forget essential life-sustaining relationships and behave in ways that have led to the ecological crisis we see today. And so Indigenous people dance the relationship of people to animals as represented in their guiding or creation stories. They represent those symbols of life in their art forms and in the things they create in daily life. These are also symbols that help them to maintain tribal identity by assisting in learning to be responsible for their essential life-affirming relationships. Such honoring and exploration of key relationships are equally reflected in the mythological complex of Indigenous story making and telling.

Relationship with Plants

In the Southwest, plants and agricultural ways of being became part of the way that Pueblo people expressed their essential relationships. Pueblo ancestors learned how to cultivate corn in many different kinds of environments and developed numerous strains of corn that were drought resistant and grew under a variety of conditions. For the Pueblo people corn became a sacrament of life, that is, a representation of life itself and the connection that Pueblo people feel towards the plant world. Corn is reflected in Pueblo art forms and in their ways of understanding themselves as a people.

Contemporary Hopi artists at times depict First Man and First Woman as perfect ears of corn being shrouded and guided by a Corn Mother who is a representation of Earth Mother.

Pueblo people express this intimate understanding and relationship by dancing for the perpetuation of corn—in June, July, and August, grand Corn Dances occur in many Pueblos in the Southwest. Indeed, until very recently, corn, beans, squash—all of the things which Pueblo people grew—were the physical foundation of Pueblo life and livelihood. These are the dances that Pueblo people maintain to the present, and they represent themselves and their reflections of each other as a community of relationship. According to one Pueblo proverb, "We are all kernels on the same corn cob."

Pueblo Journeys

Pueblo ancestors lived and hunted in New Mexico for 10,000 years or more following herds of mastodon and bison retreating from the great glaciers of the north. Those early communities of Pueblo hunter-gatherers evolved and developed as groups comprised of no more than two or three extended families living together. Through the process of utilizing everything in their environment they began to understand the nature of sustaining themselves within the environments in which they lived. They developed understandings of how to use the things around them to clothe themselves, to create baskets and pottery, and to sustain themselves in terms of food and shelter. Gradually, those communities became larger and more complex. In those larger, more complex communities, an understanding evolved that people had to honor relationship and reciprocity, not only in terms of each other, but more importantly, in the context of the environments they depended on for life.

In the stories Pueblo elders tell, the ancestors journeyed many times and settled in many places, including Chaco Canyon, Mesa Verde, and Canyon de Chelly. And each time they stopped they established a relationship to the place in which they settled, and they learned from each of these places. They came to understand something about the essence of these natural places and something about the delicate environmental balance of nature in such places. They settled by lakes and came to understand the nature of water and its importance and sanctity in an arid environment. They came to understand that water was one of the foundations for maintenance of life on earth. They settled near mountains and came to understand the nature of mountains in terms of the way they provided a context, an environment in which Pueblo people and other living things could live.

The Pueblo people have depicted this sort of ecological understanding in many forms, one of which is the symbolic mythic figure called Kokopelli. Kokopelli is the seed carrier and the creative spirit of nature's fertility, good fortune, culture, art, music, and dance. Kokopelli is a reflection of the procreative powers of nature and the creative powers of the human mind. Pueblos saw themselves as reflections of Kokopelli, as creative spirits in sacred interaction with natural places of the landscape, as bearers of natural gifts, and as planters of seeds. This spiritual ecology is linked to the Pueblos' guiding story in which the People emerged from the earth's navel at the time of creation and began to journey through a sacred landscape. At this time in the remote past, the first people came to understand the meaning of their sacred relationship to the earth and to "that place that the People talk about."

Pueblo peoples, like all Indigenous peoples, have a guiding story. According to some versions of this guiding story, humans now live in the fifth world. There were four worlds before this one, and in each of those worlds human beings had to learn something. They had to come to terms with an evolutionary task to, in a sense, become more complete as human beings. Each world metaphorically represents a stage of natural evolution through which human beings learn how to become more human. Pueblo people believe that they emerged from an earth navel, a place of mountains looked upon lovingly by the sun and the moon. It is believed that those first people were taught by certain animals, and that their thoughts were also guided by the evergreen tree of life. This was "that place that the People talk about."

Through guiding stories of creation many American Indian tribes symbolize the earth as a feminine being to whom all living things relate, and whose body follows the contours of the landscape. Indian people also represent these perceptions of life in relationship with the land in their oral traditions and through the symbols of art, ritual, and the attitudes and activities that all Indians have traditionally practiced. It is through these symbols and participating with the land in a kind of symbolic dance that Pueblo people have traditionally maintained the memory of their relationship to their places. Through traditional art forms such as pottery, which are replete with designs based on their relationship to the land, its plants, animals, Pueblo people have symbolized their sense of identity as a people of place. This continual establishing of relationship is not only for renewal and for remembering to remember who they are as a people, but is also an attempt to perpetuate the spiritual ecology of the world as a whole. This is the complex of relationship, symbolism, attitude, and way of interacting with the land that comprises the Pueblo theology of place.

Today there are still numerous communal reflections of

natural affiliation among the Pueblo people of New Mexico. The place currently called "New Mexico" is also sometimes called "the land of enchantment." For some, one reason for the evocation of a feeling of enchantment is that New Mexico has been consecrated by the lives and communities of so many Pueblo people for many centuries. New Mexico is not only a place where geological and ecological regions intersect, it is also a meeting place of ideas, cultures, and ways of community.

Indigenous Ecology in a Post-Modern World

Native people throughout the Americas developed environmentally sound ways of living with the land. Traditionally, they deeply understood and venerably practiced the concept of sustainability within a particular environment. This way of sustainable living evolved into numerous ways of maintaining harmony, both at the individual and communal level, in dynamic balance with the places in which Indian people have lived in North America. Ceremonial traditions combined with practical ecological knowledge expressed their orientation to sacred ecology and formed the basis for a theology of place.

However, American Indian people today live a dual existence. At times, it resembles a kind of schizophrenia in which people constantly try to adapt themselves to a mainstream social, political, and cultural system that is not their own. They are constantly faced with living in a larger society that does not really understand nor respect their traditional life symbols, ecological perspectives, understanding of relationship to the land, and traditional ways of remembering to remember who they are. Moreover, because of modern education and Native peoples' long-term relationships with the U.S. government, many have moved away from a practiced and conscious relationship with place, or direct connection with their spiritual ecology. The results for many Indian communities are "existential" problems, such as high rates of alcoholism, suicide, abuse of self and others, depression, and other social and spiritual ills. Tewa people call this state of schizophrenic-like existence *pingeh heh* (split thought or thinking, or doing things with only half of one's mind). As an Indian educator, I believe that modern Indian education ultimately has to be about healing this split. Healing the split is not a task for Indian people only. It is also the task of others who consider themselves people of place, and thereby experience alienation from mainstream society as do many Indian people. Today everyone must "look to the mountain."

Much of what has been presented in this essay about Native American traditions and an Indigenous ecology is an ideal image. As mentioned above, in many Native communities these traditions have undergone significant deterioration. I am reminded by a sculpture by a former Pueblo student at the Institute of American Indian Arts (Santa Fe, New Mexico). She created a clay piece that symbolized her feelings as a young Native woman attempting to be an artist and live in two worlds (trying to be traditional and also modern). The clay sculpture was an androgynous figure sitting with its arms folded; its hands wrung around each other in such a way that the entire form expressed extreme anxiety. To extend this sculptural metaphor of anxiety, the head of the figure had been split in half. Half of the face was drawn up in a smile, and the other half drawn down in a frown. The artist's deeply felt sense of being split, torn as she was between diametrically opposed world views, captures the sense of fragmentation and the dilemma that we all face as modern people living in an ecologically schizophrenic world. The young artist felt a sense of "splitedness" and incompleteness.

My sense as an educator is that Indigenous education must now focus on the recovery of Native peoples' sensibility for natural affiliation and nurturance of this sensibility in their children. The education of the twenty-first century must be about healing this cultural and ecological split. Once again, healing this schizophrenia is not just the task of Indigenous education, but the task of all education. Our quintessential educational task is that of reconnecting with our innate sense and need for natural affiliation.

Human interactive relationships with places give rise to and define human cultures and communities. As we change our landscape and allow the self-serving will of materialist economic systems to have sway over our view of the land, we also allow the natural landscape of mind and soul to be altered in the same measure. When we allow school curricula to serve the will of the "marketplace," we also allow the landscape of students' minds to be altered. The price we pay for such lack of consciousness in school curricula is incalculable. Indeed, with each generation since the turn of the century, Americans have collectively become more materially affluent. Yet, at the same time each generation of Americans has become significantly more impoverished in terms of collective and individual connection to places that form the biological and geographic tapestry of America.

We must once again ask the perennial question, "What is education for?" Our collective answer to this ancient question carries with it consequences that are more profound now than ever before in the history of humankind. It is important to move beyond the idealization and patronization of Indigenous knowledge, which often leads to marginalization of the most profound Indigenous ways of knowing how human beings and nature interact. Indigenous people must be supported in their collective attempts to restore their traditions while also recreating and revitalizing themselves in ways they feel are appropriate in contemporary society.

Indigenous people have been touted as the spiritual leaders of the environmental movement. Such a designation is more symbolic than tangible since most environmental education is still primarily a reaction to the shortcomings of mainstream Western education. Still, many environmental educators, writers, and philosophers advocate getting back to the basics of relationship to environment and also to each other within communities, thereby paralleling the traditional practices of Indigenous societies. This is appropriate since Indigenous people around the world have much to share and much to give. The same peoples also continue to be among the most exploited and oppressed, and are usually the people who suffer the greatest loss of self and culture when dealing with various economic development and educational schemes. In spite of this, Indigenous groups around the world have a very important message, a message that is related in a number of ways to the evolving disciplines of eco-psychology and eco-philosophy.

>>>→ • ←<<<

As we begin our journeys to find the Indigenous mind-set that will allow for sustainable (and even restorative) ways of living at all levels, we must think about who we are and who we represent. Understand that each of us in our own small way is a vital link within the context of creating and remembering the reciprocal relationships that sustain and enliven the earth, flora and fauna, and human beings—in brief, local to global ecology. Whether the role you play is large or small, know that it has an effect. As you look to and imagine climbing the primordial mountain, reflect on your own life and understanding of what it means to be educated and intelligent. As you move from the mountain down a pathway to resume your journey guided by ecological thought and action, think about the journey of your life in relationship to a "place." It is the task of each of us to "look to the mountain" and build a vision of a sustainable future for the people inhabiting Mother Earth in the year 2000, 3000, and beyond.

2

Nourishing Gifts
Native and Traditional Foods of the Southwestern Pueblos

Brett M. Bakker

The *"three sisters"*—corn, beans, and squash. Photograph © Brett Bakker, Native Seeds/SEARCH.

The Pueblo Diet

"Eat good." Used as an invitation, a blessing, and a bidding to eat your fill (and then some more), these words are often heard in Pueblo households while seated at the table for Feast Day. During the celebration, the Catholic patron saint of the village is honored by dancers and by the feeding of family, friends, neighbors, and total strangers.

There's little enough room at the table to actually eat, packed as it is with serving bowls of steaming green chile stew, perhaps with *chicos* (reconstituted smoky green corn) or *calabacitas* (young and tender squash); two kinds of red chile (one thick and meaty, the other thin with mutton bones); *posole* (hominy corn stew); beans (pintos or, at the northern Pueblos, garbanzos); white bread freshly baked in the *horno* (outdoor adobe oven) and sometimes *pansa* or *capriotada* (sweet bread pudding dotted with raisins and cheese); *tamales* (especially around the winter holidays); red chile, cheese *enchiladas* made with flour *tortillas* rather than corn; and occasionally, deer or elk stew with no chile or spices, just the good flavor of wild meat. All of these dishes are more or less the traditional diet in Pueblo households. Cuisine that is usually called Mexican in New Mexico is actually the blend of cooking styles of Pueblo Indians and Spanish settlers. This cuisine is hearty and nourishing but low in nonstarchy vegetables.

But you will also find many other dishes that have become traditional in recent decades: cakes; pies; the ubiquitous Jello, brightly colored and mixed with marshmallows or artificial whipped cream; candies; and lots of coffee, soda pop, and over-sweetened instant drinks to wash it all down. Just about the only nonstarchy vegetables around are skimpy iceberg lettuce salads or diced broccoli, cauliflower, and carrots mixed with mayonnaise, and even these are rather sparse in terms of quantity.

Low fiber and high levels of fat, starch, salt, and sugar make for filling meals, but also lack balanced nutrition. The most problematic aspect of Native American nutrition (as well as for Australian Aboriginals and Pacific Islanders) is the extremely high percentage of adult-onset diabetes. The modern high-calorie diet, however much based on tradition, is a contributing factor to diabetes, as are low levels of exercise. Studies suggest that Indian metabolisms, evolved over time in the context of the desert's feast/famine cycle, helped the people to survive by storing calories as body fat, which was used as needed. Now these extra calories are not used and contribute to Type II (noninsulin dependent) diabetes, which is common among Native peoples.

Individuals with diabetes should avoid sharp increases in blood sugar. Food must be evenly digested so as to not aggravate the pancreas, the human insulin-producing organ. Complex carbohydrate foods with large amounts of amylase fiber are desirable in the diet. These soluble fibers form gels which slow absorption. Insoluble fibers such as bran, while necessary for balanced meals, do not act in the same way. Soluble fiber permits food to be slowly digested over a four- to six-hour period instead of one or two hours.

Ordinary beans *(Phaseolus vulgaris)* fall somewhere in between soluble and insoluble fibers, but tepary beans *(P. acutifolius)* are even better. Not unsurprisingly, teparies are native to the most extreme arid lands of North America, that is, the Sonoran Desert, home to the Tohono O'odham and Pima tribes whose rates of diabetes are close to fifty percent. Just as these desert peoples are efficient in storing calories, the teparies are well adapted to the harsh environment. They withstand and even thrive in temperatures exceeding 105° F. Their roots delve fifty percent deeper in search of moisture than the common bean. Unlike ordinary species, tepary yields decline with excess moisture. Perhaps the most remarkable aspect of these plants is their ability to germinate in relatively dry ground, and to use moisture rapidly and efficiently. Tepary beans actually keep leaf temperature and vapor transpiration high, racing toward reproduction at a rate that would shut down circulatory processes in response to excess heat in their common cousins. Tepary beans also contain higher percentages of calcium, iron, and usable proteins. Consequently, this food complements the Native corn-based diet, corn being low in total usable proteins. But beans seem to have fallen out of favor at the table, and with the exception of a few notable examples, corn seems to be more important in the context of traditional religious belief than traditional diet.

What Makes a Food Traditional?

Some foods introduced to the Pueblos have an interesting way of becoming traditional. For example, prune pies (actually more of a pastry) have been around since the Spanish introduced plums and wheat. They aren't seen much, even in traditional Spanish households, but they're still around at the Pueblos. The pies are made from prune filling between thin layers of crust made of white flour, sugar, and shortening. All four ingredients are included in U.S. Department of Agriculture commodity foods distributed on the reservations. What else are you going to do with a dozen boxes of prunes? Anglos introduced dough deep fried in lard as quick and easy camp fare, but fry bread persists as "traditional Indian food"—again, wheat flour and lard were and continue to be commodity foods.

Availability of a food as well as the technology to process the food are also factors in dietary choices. For example, tortillas are Indian food through and through. Most Native peoples the world over have some form of flatbread, but corn flatbread is uniquely American. The Spanish introduced wheat flour as an alternative to corn: high gluten content meant easy tortilla making, and wheat is planted and harvested off season from Native crops and needs less care. (This was an early conflict between the two peoples. The Spanish view was that a fall-planted, spring/winter tended, and early summer harvested crop—especially a staple to the Spaniards—would keep the Native people busy, thereby teaching them a lesson in European industriousness. The Pueblos were accustomed to hunting at these times as well as performing ceremonies and looking inwards with storytelling—essential to the continuance of tradition—that busy summers would not allow. Consequently, initial reluctance from the Pueblos to raise wheat was based on worldview as much or more than simple dietary preference, and not at all on sloth.) Again, abundant commodity and store-bought flour eased corn out as a tortilla staple, as well as the early Spanish demand for wheat from the tribes as part of the *encomienda* or tribute system. Although corn is still revered at the Pueblos and used as ceremonial meal, as well as in posole, chicos, and tamales, wheat is the principal grain consumed in the form of oven bread.

In the rare instances when tortillas are still made by Pueblo women, they are always of wheat flour—unlike the corn tortillas made by rural Indian women of Mexico who have little money to buy wheat flour and poor access even if they can spare the expense. Wheat grows better in more northern climates, and even if Mexicans could raise it, how would poor *campesinas* mill wheat and separate bran and germ without modern machinery?[1] Mano and metate stones are not as effective for grinding wheat; they were made for softer corn.

The European practice of discarding the most nutritious part of the wheat (which often ends up as livestock feed) and consuming the relatively nutrient-poor endosperm (white flour) was invented in the name of gentility and longer shelf life. Native technology, however, is perfectly suited to processing corn for maximum nutritional potential.

Tortillas are not made of whole dry cornmeal—the flatbread would readily fall apart and taste much different—but rather from easily ground cooked corn. The grain is first boiled in lime or ash, and each individual kernel's shell removed by washing. Used as is for posole, this processed food *(nixtamal* in Nahuatl) is ground wet and made into a dough for tortillas or tamales (meat and chile-filled dough, wrapped in cornhusks and baked). Unlike other processed grains, this processed corn is actually higher in nutrition because the action of the lime complements the protein content of the grain. This change in the balance of proteins is effected by the use of alkalis such as slaked lime (calcium hydroxide) or plant ashes (potassium hydroxide, usually from juniper, chamisa or three-wing saltbush—*Juniperus spp., Artemesia tridentata,* and *Atriplex canescens,* respectively).

Certain amino acids (the building blocks of protein) are

not so much absent in corn, but unavailable as nutrients unless a catalyst is present. A particular amino is available only in proportion to the other aminos present; that is, if one amino is present in only a small amount, the availability of the others is limited to the same amount. Balance is key to accessibility of aminos as food.

For example, two proteins found in corn—zein and glutelin—are unbalanced by the low content of the aminos lysine and tryptophan. An added alkali changes that balance, thereby increasing the total nutrients available from the grain. Niacin, an amino essential for cell metabolic processes, is also low in corn. Since the body can use tryptophan to make niacin, increasing the former also enhances the latter.

In the case of blue corn, where the color has historically been considered as important as the food, ash is added directly to the cooking mush made from whole unprocessed corn. Changes in acid content or heat affect color; alkali raises the pH, thereby preserving color as well as enhancing nutrition.

In these ways, even a sparse diet of mainly corn is optimized. The grain is prepared in dozens of ways without sacrificing quality on any level. Contrast this with poor Anglos of the Dust Bowl days living on lard-fried whole cornmeal cakes and contracting pellagra (skin and mouth sores and general weakness) from a deficient diet.

Corn as Food, Blessing, and Gift

When a people has one staple they count on, year in and year out, they soon devise every way possible to prepare it. Indians throughout the Americas shared similar ways of serving corn. Judging by the archaeological record and their oral traditions, the Indigenous peoples had quite a long time to develop these processes. The earliest evidence of corn as a domesticate shows up about 5000 BC in Mexico, although theories and dates are often revised. When a piece of archaeological evidence points to a certain era, it's assumed that there was a preceding period during which the material evidence became widespread.

By the oral traditions of Southwest tribes, corn is a gift from the Creator through intermediaries. This is all the more intriguing when corn is compared to the world's other staple grains. Indeed, all traditional peoples have similar stories for wheat, rice, and so on. The difference is that with the exception of corn, ethnobotany can point to wild ancestors that have led directly to the domesticates for all other staple grains.

Although plants such as Job's Tears *(Coix jacobi)* or the grass *Tricapsum* have been suggested as gene contributors, there is no direct wild progenitor of corn. Teosinte *(Zea diploperennis,* quite closely related to corn, *Zea mays)* was once considered corn's forerunner. It is now known to have been "merely" a major gene donor, a plant capable of cross-pollination with corn. In parts of Mexico where teosinte appears as a cornfield weed, a few plants are allowed to stand in the fields and are recognized by some tribes as beneficial to the corn (by hybridization, it adds vigor to the crop). Although somewhat lankier in appearance, teosinte is easily recognized as a corn relative. To the unfamiliar eye it can be indistinguishable until it produces progeny. Unlike corn that bears female silks along the stalk and male tassels above, teosinte delivers both pollen and seed atop the plant. Most striking is that ears of teosinte are not covered in a husk.

Huskless ears are advantageous in terms of swift and easy seed dispersal. An ear of corn wrapped in layers of leafy husk is advantageous from a human perspective, in that the food is protected from birds, rodents, and some insects. An ear of corn falling to the earth cannot naturally disperse seed because hundreds of sprouts choke each other beneath the husk. Is there a missing link of sorts between teosinte (the wild) and corn (the cultivated)? No other cultivated crop has a mechanism so favorable to the farmer.

One ancient variety is pod corn, throwbacks of which are occasionally seen among the oldest corn varieties that still exist. There is a husk around each seed on the small cobs, much like most wild grains. However, a direct link to a wild progenitor for corn has not yet been discovered, which indicates a long history of a mutually beneficial relationship between people and plant. From the standpoint of Indian tradition, which may not recognize plant science, the absence of a direct link corresponds to the Indian belief of corn being given directly to humans for their benefit. It's no wonder then that corn is important as a staple, as well as holding an important mythic place in Native culture. The people and the corn are often seen as one.

Through people's long association with corn, then, many ways were devised to serve the grain. These culinary practices also relate directly to five types of corn that developed in differing climates—pop, flint, dent, flour, and sweet. The popcorn type, characterized by small ears and seeds, is archaeologically the oldest (pod corn is also a popcorn). When heated, the extremely hard seed husk causes pressure to build in the grain until it explodes or pops. Popcorn may be ground for meal but its hard coat makes this more labor intensive. The flint and dent corn types are also hard, and are found among the northern tribes of what is now the United States. These types perform better at higher elevations than the soft flour corns of the Southwest. Sweet corn was not unknown among the North American tribes but was not accorded the status it now has as a vegetable.

What Native American cultures know well and the general populace does not, is that flour corn may be eaten in the green or immature stage, as in the case of sweet corn. While still in the husk, the ear is soaked in water and slowly roasted in a fire's embers. These are known as *elotes* in Mexican Spanish.

Carrying the process a step further, the Pueblos roast dozens or hundreds of ears, unsoaked but still in the husk, in pits or the horno overnight. The results have a smoked caramel flavor. Some of the corn is eaten the following day, but most is set to dry, hung by the peeled-back husk. The kernels dry rock hard and store with little or no pest problem. Ears may be reconstituted and cooked whole, or the grain shelled from the cob and boiled as chicos, usually with meat and chile. Besides offering a different way to eat corn, this is a way to use immature corn threatened by early frost. A traditional Navajo treat called kneel-down bread is made of grated green corn wrapped like a tamale in corn husks and baked to cake-like consistency.

Mature dry corn processed in alkali yields hominy-like *nixtamal* and produces posole, or when ground wet, yields *masa,* which is formed into tortillas or tamale dough. Dry corn also yields cornmeal of varying fineness, depending on the grinding stones and expertise of the miller. Especially important as an offering/blessing during Pueblo ceremonials, cornmeal is also used in many dishes. Meal is made into various stovetop breadstuffs, panbreads, and dumplings. Depending on the amount of water used and time cooked, porridge and drinks are made, such as *atole* and *chaquegue.* Whole dry corn can be parched in pots filled with clean dry sand (to ensure even cooking) for the forerunner of modern "cornnut" snacks.

Dry corn is also toasted and then finely ground to be used as *pinole;* pinole is either eaten as is or mixed with water for quick nourishment. This was once a very important food on extended hunting trips where traveling light was essential. It's important to note that pinole can also be made from sweet mesquite pods or any combination of wild gathered seeds, such as amaranths or lambsquarters.

In contemporary usage, sugar may sometimes be added to pinole or desserts that call for cornmeal. While at the Hopi village of Walpi, I was invited to eat at a household of complete strangers after I discovered that their neighbor, my friend, was not in. After a meal of mutton and chile stews, I was offered a pudding-like dessert. A bucket had been lined with corn husks and filled with a batter of cornmeal and sugar. The covered bucket was baked underground until the contents were solid enough to grab by the handful, but still soft, much like Italian cornmeal polenta.

One of my favorite treats, however, is to pick an ear of green corn just as the day is warming and sit beneath the plant while eating the sweet new kernels. During a long day working in the fields, this is a true gift.

Old and New World Legumes

As mentioned previously, beans of any kind are much neglected in the modern Pueblo diet. Among the dozens of homes I've visited over a twenty-year period, only two or three have served beans with any regularity. This is particularly striking when we constantly hear of the Native triumvirate of corn, squash, and beans, which go well together in the field and on the table.

We are told that corn plants provide poles for beans to climb as they in turn provide nitrogen to nourish the corn stalks, while squash plants spread out below, acting as a moisture-retaining living mulch. Beans also provide the protein complement to get the most of the corn's nutrition, while squash provides vitamins and other vegetable-derived nutrients such as carotene. If such complementarity is accurate, why then isn't the trio found together anymore in Pueblo fields or tables?

Although my observations are not exhaustive nor comprehensive, I have rarely seen beans planted during my visits to most of the Pueblos. (Hopi is the hands-down winner, however, in terms of planting beans.) But even when beans are raised, they are planted alone in a field as are corn, chile, and so on. This practice is due to the infiltration of the modern mentality of row-cropping monoculture or traditions of flood irrigation where unruly rows or to beds impede water flow. In addition, the use of tractors requires an elementary linear layout in order to move efficiently in the field.

I have tried planting corn, beans, and squash together. The results? The beans were spindly and bore little because they were over-shaded by the corn. The corn did well but was almost impossible to get to without trampling squash plants—not yet producing—that had spread to cover every row. I believe simple inefficiency is the key to why this planting arrangement is not common. In addition, most beans found in the Southwest are not necessarily climbers, but act instead as "twiners"; they are more like vines than bush beans, but will hold their own abbreviated vines aloft.

Southwestern farmers, however, do rotate corn, beans, and

squash in the same fields. What was a corn field one year may be planted to squash for a season before being planted to beans for several years. This arrangement works well and makes the best use of the plants' complementary feeding habits. Data about agricultural practices of the Mandans (of the Dakota territories) provide a clue about planting of the triumvirate elsewhere. It has been noted that corn and beans were planted in alternating rows. These were then reversed the following season for purposes of soil conservation.

Explaining why beans (and squash for that matter) are rarely served at mealtimes among the Pueblos is much more elusive. The most constant legume seen at Pueblos, and mostly the Tewa Pueblos at that, is the garbanzo *(Cicer arietinum)*. It's interesting that garbanzos are served mostly at the northern Pueblos where Spanish contact has been the most consistent. Garbanzos were one of the few Old World legumes introduced by the Spanish. Peas *(Pisum sativum)*, fava bean*s (Vicia faba)*, and lentils *(Lens esculentum)* were also introduced by the Spanish, but all three are rarely raised today in Pueblo fields.

The complementarity of tepary beans and corn has already been mentioned, but the common *Phaseolus vulgaris* bean fits here as well. Twenty to thirty percent protein is not uncommon, but protease inhibitors and lectins in the bean itself keep the human body from utilizing all crude protein. Cooking reduces these inhibitors but does not eliminate them. Consequently, eating corn complements the beans in terms of usable proteins. Also found in common beans are fat levels of only one to two percent, and respectable levels of calcium, iron, magnesium, phosphorus, zinc, and vitamins B^1, B^2, and niacin.

Nevertheless, outside of Mexico, beans are a very minor part of the Southwest Indian diet. Even Arizona's Tohono

O'odham—once known as the Papago, a Spanish corruption of another tribe's word for them, the "Bean Eaters"—consume fewer and fewer beans. New Mexicans of Spanish ancestry eat many more legumes than Indigenous New Mexicans. The archaeological records suggest that beans were domesticated later than corn, probably around 4000 BC at the earliest. In the Southwest, there is a bit of evidence to suggest that beans were introduced less than 2000 years after corn. Still, thousands of intervening years would be enough time to acquire a serious bean habit. Corn is, however, much easier to grow than beans and has fewer serious pests in Pueblo country, as well as having greater ceremonial significance. These factors may partly explain the rarity of beans served at meals, but I suspect also that the easy availability of once scarce meat is also responsible.

Good Meat

Meat is a preferred and very large part of the Pueblo diet and wild meat seems prized most of all. I once drove a Pueblo friend to the supermarket. She wanted to shop for food to bring home when she returned to the reservation for Christmas. The shopping cart was literally half full of meat—steaks, chops, ground beef, chicken, cubed pork, and more—for a few days' visit. On occasion, I've been treated to deer or elk jerky (from the Spanish *charqui*) while at certain dances. A game stew on the table along with other Feast Day fare is also common. But I was unprepared for what occurred when I stopped in to visit a Pueblo family with a gift of firewood for their past hospitality.

My friend, the father of the family, was not in, but I met one of his sons. After unloading the wood, he mentioned that he'd shot a deer earlier that morning. Not being a hunter, I attempted to ask the most intelligent questions possible. He answered readily and, as an afterthought, asked if I'd like some meat to take home. I replied that I'd be glad to have some and would pick it up whenever it was convenient. Even I realized that the deer would not yet have been butchered.

I was then led into the living room, where the deer lay on expensive Pendleton blankets flecked with blood. Going into the kitchen, he returned with two carving knives, handed me one, and bent over the deer and began to skin it at the front leg. Feeling quite useless, I crouched nearby. I wasn't squeamish but truly had no idea what to do. Just then the phone rang. He handed me his knife saying, "You finish up," and left the room. I halfheartedly imitated his lifting the skin with the knife. Fortunately for me, a cousin entered the house and began talking, which gave me an opportunity to stop what I was doing. When the cousin left the room, the son returned and resumed the task. When that portion of hide was free of the flesh, he cut some meat free, and then interrupted himself.

"I almost forgot," he said, and reached into the animal (the deer was already gutted). I heard a muffled snap. His hand emerged holding the liver. He held it to me.

"Take a bite. It's what we do [before butchering]." I did. The meat was warm—softer and tastier than I thought it would be. He was pleased; he'd assumed I would be queasy or nervous. I think I may have proved myself to him somehow. (This experience reminded me of an incident a few years before when I was passed Indian-grown tobacco and corn husks at a neighboring Pueblo. The adults present grinned in anticipation and the little kids laughed and pointed, but they were all surprised that I could roll a cigarette and light it without missing a beat in the conversation.)

The entire front leg—hoof and all—was presented to me. I was told not to cook it with chile or spices but to prepare it simply. As I drove away, I felt blessed to participate, even in a small way, in such a special event. The deer being transformed into food for humans was accorded special treatment, but because taking game was also considered such a common event, it was assumed that I had the skills to dress the carcass.

As a farming people, the Pueblos had little time and manpower to spare for hunting until the fall when the harvest was safely in. The best and biggest game was found at the higher elevations, some distance away from the warm agricultural valleys. Cattle, goats, and sheep introduced by the Spanish were welcome, especially multi-use sheep (although they were in some ways better suited to the nomadic Navajo and Apaches). Even in dry years when the rivers failed to bring sufficient water for crops, livestock could be driven to higher elevations where decent pasture was available.

In any case, meat provides more to the modern Pueblo diet than plants. There is a significant relationship here. In Pueblo culture, animals are closely related to humans in ways not recognized by modern biology. While attempting to explain my vegetarianism (long since abandoned after years at the Pueblos) to a friend from Taos, he shook his head. "We eat animals," he said simply, "because they are part of us."

Chile as Staple and Condiment

At the risk of challenging prevailing anthropological theories based on available archeological data, I question the assertion that chiles were introduced from Mexico to the American Southwest by the Spanish. It seems strange that Pueblos, who regularly traded with their southern neighbors for copper bells, macaw feathers, and so forth, would be unfamiliar with the crop, let alone never attempting, as a farming people, to raise it themselves. With that personal observation out of the way, the record on chile *(Capsicum annuum* and related species) stands as follows.

The area of greatest diversity of wild chiles (i.e., probable center of origin) has been located anywhere from central Bolivia to Brazil's southern mountains. Chiles are assumed to have spread, depending on species, to different locations. All were once perennial shrubs bearing small fingernail-size fruits with high levels of heat produced by capsaicin, the chemical found mostly along the seed-bearing placental tissue. A dilution of as low as one part capsaicin per 100,000 is perceptible on the human tongue. However, it does not actually burn but rather stimulates pain receptors in the mouth. The main dispersal agents of chiles in the wild are birds whose mouths do not contain the proper pain receptors. They are attracted by the bright red mature fruits. Birds will eagerly feed on them, depositing seed presoftened by their digestive tracts into suitable places, each encapsulated within their droppings, which act as an initial fertilizer.

The earliest archaeological record associated with humans is about 7000 BC in Mexico. Well before 3000 BC, larger fruits (i.e., domesticated forms) were appearing. By the time of the Spanish conquest, there were dozens of forms approaching the sizes we are familiar with today.

More important than size, however, is the development of traits that make chiles easier to grow for humans. Wild chiles are borne erect on their stems where birds can feed on them with ease. Domesticates bear pendant pods that could be hidden by foliage, thereby discouraging avian feeding. As with most uncultivated plants, chile fruits mature rapidly and drop readily from the mother plant for successful seed dispersal. Chile cultivars with larger fleshier pods remain attached longer, thereby permitting extended opportunities for harvest (in ripe and unripe stages) as well as offering further discouragement from bird predations.

Perhaps the most important aspect of chile cultivars is their flower structure. This structure made it more difficult for insects to reach the pollen. Because the flower structure encourages self-pollination, it diminishes crossbreeding and has kept the new varieties relatively pure.

But to chile eaters, the range of varietal characteristics is vital. For different sauces and salsas, sun and smoke drying or plain fresh eating, the range of tastes and uses is staggering. Meaty *jalapeño* and *serrano* types do not dry readily, but smoking them yields a flavorful product that can be reconstituted in any number of ways. *Pasilla* types dry when mature to a dark brown; they are used in Mexican *moles*, that is, prepared with unsweetened chocolate into a rich sauce typically served over chicken or turkey.

The most well-known chiles in the Southwest are the New Mexico (formerly Anaheim) types which can be either roasted and peeled green or allowed to mature and then sun dried to a deep red. The peeled green freezes well, and traditionally was dried whole or pounded to a pulp that was spread on smooth rocks set in the sun. Along with the red, the peeled green has long been used in the familiar meaty Pueblo stews. Red chile pods are most often reconstituted and ground or milled dry into powder, then is made into the sauces used in many New Mexican dishes. In fact, what has for some time been popularly called Mexican food (e.g., *enchiladas* and *chiles rellenos)* is a blend of Pueblo and colonial Spanish cuisines. In many parts of Mexico, chiles appear in uncooked salsas or thin sauces, the most familiar being the commercially bottled Tabasco sauce. As the popularity of chiles increase (salsa now outsells tomato catsup), extra pungent species are gaining in popularity. The fiery yet fruity *habanero (Capsicum chinensis)*, probably of Yucatán origin, has been touted as the very hottest. In fact, there are hotter varieties, wild and cultivated, that have yet to be marketed outside of Bolivia.

It is worth noting that chile consumption is concentrated in the warmer regions of the world (e.g., the desert and tropical Americas, and Sichuan China). At first, one would think that people in colder climes would welcome warming foods. But, in addition to the fact that chiles grow best in warm climates (being perennial in frost-free areas), they act as a coolant for the human body. Copious perspiration evaporates quickly in warm surroundings, dropping skin temperatures even as the mouth "burns." And as all who eat chiles know, water does not necessarily relieve the burning sensation. Water cannot dilute the capsaicin, and thus only temporarily gives the sensation of cooling. The resumption of the volatile oil's effects can then seem redoubled. Starchy foods are somewhat effective at reducing the burning sensation, but only high fat foods such as milk or cheese are effective, because oils are most proficient at cutting other oils.

Besides the celebrated "high" that leaves the diner ready for more even as the hottest bites have barely faded, chile nutrients are also craved by the body. The vitamin C content of chiles is similar to that of most citrus fruits, and carotene is found in amounts equal to that of carrots. Vitamins P, E, and B complexes are also found in high amounts. To the modern diet, currently low in vitamin-rich fresh foods, this is indeed a good addition, especially to Native Americans and other chile aficionados who include the fiery food at nearly every meal.

Pueblo and Mesoamerican Greens and (Pseudo) Grains

The absence of fresh greens at each meal is a contemporary phenomenon. Many wild leafy species (falling under the Spanish catchall *quelites*) were once seasonally gathered and served in large quantities.

Various Amaranthus species have been gathered, cultivated, and/or encouraged by people the world over. Amaranth can be segregated into two types: those most suitable for greens (e.g., black-seeded *A. palmeri, A. retroflexus, A. gangeticus*) and others more appropriate for grain (e.g., blond-seeded *A. hypochondriacus, A. cruentes*).

Among the vegetable types, leaves from young plants are more nutritious than amaranth relatives spinach, chard, and beet tops. High in calories, vitamins A and C, calcium, iron, niacin, and riboflavin, amaranth has been called the meat of the poor. In the United States, amaranth species are more well known as pigweed—fed to swine or vigorously eradicated from the garden. They are prevalent in garden or disturbed soils, due in part to outstanding growth performance. Amaranth is a member of a select group of plants known to have what is called C4 metabolism. Carbon dioxide is essential to photosynthesis, but is lost through plant pores as they open to feed the process. C4 plants store carbon dioxide where vapor loss is low until it can be used. Unit for unit, amaranth needs half the water for twice the plant growth of non-C4 plants. They are also highly efficient in using desert light levels by tracking the sun's angle for maximum solar gain. And while certain greens do accumulate oxalates (that tie up otherwise digestible calcium) and nitrates in rates high enough for concern, desert amaranth species levels are low and, with a typical serving, well within safety zones for humans.

Among the Hopi villages of Arizona, a black-seeded *A. cruentes* called *komo* yields deep burgundy leaves and seed bracts. Although the leaves are eaten in their early stages, it is the bracts that are prized most for making a scarlet food dye. *Piki* is a paper-thin corn "bread" made by swiping a handful of batter over a glassy-smooth heated stone made for just this purpose. Komo is among a handful of natural dyes used for ceremonial or secular piki. These uses (as well as other ceremonial purposes) are not restricted to Arizona, but were also common among the Rio Grande Pueblos of New Mexico where pockets of usage remain.

The shiny dark seeds of the red *cruentes* and more common green-leaved *A. retroflexus* have been eaten alone or mixed with other wild seeds as a porridge, but it is the blond-seeded, Mexican types (now relatively rare among continental U.S. tribes) that are best for this use. Although not a true grain (in the sense of seeds produced by grasses), amaranth outperforms all the world's staple seeds, weighing in at 16 percent total protein with high lysine content, as compared to a lysine-lacking 12 to 14 percent for corn, rice, wheat, and so on. Its calcium, iron, phosphorus, riboflavin, and ascorbic acid content is also generally higher.

Thriving in marginal lands, which in itself is enough to distinguish the plant, grain amaranths are noteworthy for their yields: they can produce over 50,000 seeds per plant. Cooked whole as grain, ground for flour or meal, or popped for confections, amaranth is a versatile food. It was so important to Mesoamerican cultures (including the Maya, but particularly the Aztec or Mexica) that amaranth was noted in both Native and Spanish historical documents as a more important tribute crop than the corn required from the peasantry by the ruling classes.

Controlling the Indians' food supply was part of the Spaniards' conquest strategy. But what led the *conquistadores* to attempt total eradication of amaranth was its vital ceremonial use among certain Aztec tribes. Milled or popped grain was mixed with human blood and fed to the priests and sometimes the general populace. The fervently Catholic invaders perceived this as a blasphemy of their Holy Communion and meted out severe punishment for farming amaranth. Fields and granaries were burned and growers were subject to execution or amputation of hands.

As a result, amaranth growing went underground along with associated rituals, and its use dropped out of sight for hundreds of years. As recently as the 1960s when Rodale Institute researchers (of *Organic Gardening* magazine fame) sought to recover and reintroduce amaranth seed strains, they were met by blank stares from the original farmers' descendants. Many Natives were truly ignorant of the crop, but others knew that this knowledge was not to be shared with outsiders. A few generations is a short time in Indian minds.

A small revival in the health food market notwithstanding, amaranth usage among nontraditional cultures remains low. More palatable to some is the other great pseudocereal of the *Chenopodiaceae/Amaranthaceae* alliance, the South American

mother grain *Chenopodium quinua.* Quinua is closely related
to the edible weed *Chenopodium album* or lambsquarters, also
known as pigweed. A most important food for the Inca peoples
(Quechua and Aymara speakers), the nutritional profile of
quinua (or popularly quinoa) is comparable to amaranth: 14
to 18 percent protein, exceptionally high lysine, plus other
amino acids, methionine and crystine. In addition, quinua
contains large amounts of iron, calcium, phosphorus, and vitamins E and B complexes. Essential fatty acids comprise about
6 to 7 percent of quinua, which is unusual for a nonoilseed
food crop. Leaves of quinua and the related weedy Chenopodium can be used in much the same way as amaranth, and with
similar flavor and nutrition.

Although a better tasting grain than amaranth, there are a
few obstacles to quinua's widespread acceptance. First, unlike
amaranth, it remains a high-elevation crop. (The majority of
varieties perform best at over 7,000 feet and some at elevations
approaching 9,000.) There are only a few areas in the United
States suited to quinua as a commercial crop. In contrast, amaranth can be raised in many areas unsuited for anything else.
Second, serious U.S. research of quinua varieties, although
ongoing for well over fifteen years, has been slow. Lastly, processing is more intensive. Each quinua seed has a natural coat-
ing of saponin, a soapy compound that tastes bitter, including
to birds and insects. The saponin must be washed off before the
grain can be consumed by humans.

Returning to the Southwest, many wild greens were gathered and eaten but perhaps none so important as Rocky Mountain beeweed *(Cleome serrulata)* or *guaco* in Spanish (after the
Native term). Guaco's importance is borne out by its being
named in Pueblo ceremonial song along with only three other

plants—corn, squash, and cotton, the Pueblos' most crucial cultivars. Harvested in early spring, guaco was boiled in water, which was changed numerous times to remove its alkaline flavor. It could then be stewed with meat or corn. In some cases, guaco was boiled until it resembled a black paste. With the fibers removed, cakes of this paste were set to dry in the sun. Soaked in water and fried, it was eaten with or without condiments. These cakes were kept against lean times and some tribes claim to have weathered famine with them when winter stores had run out and greens were not yet available. Although analyses are scarce, it appears that Cleome is of great enough nutritional value to sustain humans even with extensive cooking and processing. Interestingly enough, these same cakes of guaco provided another staple for the Pueblo people: black paint (like an ink block) used on white-slip pottery.

Guaco was often served with another potherb, *Cymopterus fendleri*, called *chimaja* in Spanish (after the Tewa *tsi'maja*). In the same family as celery, it has a similar but more pronounced flavor. Picked only in the early spring (it flowers and seeds quickly), chimaja is dried and used in various dishes. I had only been familiar with it as a spice until eating a meal at Santo Domingo Pueblo. An elder, the father of the extended family I was visiting, sat beside me. He alone out of the dozen people in the house was served a thin porridge of blue cornmeal. Noticing some green vegetable in his bowl, I asked what he was eating, suspecting its identity from the celery-like aroma. He replied simply that it was good and called his daughter to serve some to me. She first asked to make sure that I wanted such food—not something anyone else in the family but an elder would want, let alone an outsider. My answer was an emphatic yes. Such a simple dish of chimaja and cornmeal was very satisfying to me, although I could have eaten much more than the small portions served to myself and the old man.

I have yet to encounter a nutritional analysis of chimaja, but I will hazard a guess based on a few points. Thin cornmeal gruels have always been fed to the very young or old as a sustaining meal of low bulk. While many elders prefer "the old foods," this was the first time that I'd seen this herb served after visiting this family over a fifteen-year period and being fed dozens of times. Though I preferred not to ask my hosts, my assumption is that, besides being a tasty dish, chimaja is suited for nourishing the aging.

Among many other formerly prevalent wild greens I've yet to see served at Pueblo feasts are desert mallows (*Sphaeralcea spp.* is also used for curling the hair as well as hardening mud floors and casts!); *verdolagas* or purslane (*Portulaca spp.*); and various mustards (*Brassica spp.*), the last mostly introduced as camp-follower weeds by Europeans. Historically, wild greens were generally eaten in quantity during their harvest season. The greens dried and stored most often for winter use were considered special—multi-use guaco or aromatic chimaja. Pigweed types, while dehydrated in small amounts for the table, were sometimes dried in quantity as hay for livestock. Drying, incidentally, neutralizes any possible excess nitrates or oxylates.

The dearth of fresh greenery consumed by contemporary Native Americans is often lamented by nutritionists. However, it should be kept in mind that the small amount of fresh vegetables in the diet parallels that of the average American citizen.

Squash, Pumpkins, and Gourds:
Seed, Flesh, and Shell

Wild gourds and humans go back as far as 7000 BC, but evidence of domesticated squashes or pumpkins has been found in association with the earliest corn in the Southwest, around 3500 BC. Botanically speaking, there is no difference between the terms squash and pumpkin. All mature fruit of the edible species of *Cucurbita* raised in the Americas can be rightly called pumpkins, especially large storage types. It is only relatively recently that small varieties of winter squash were developed. In the past, there was no use for small table varieties, good for a serving or two. When you have a community or large family to feed, squashes of individual serving size are more trouble to raise, store, and process. A ten- to thirty-pound (or larger) pumpkin yields more flesh, more seed and, in some cases, shells for utilitarian purposes.

Four major species of Cucurbita planted in the Americas are described below.

C. pepo—Of the four, these varieties are most familiar to the general public. All commercial summer squashes (e.g., yellow, crookneck, and zucchini) and most small winter squashes (e.g., acorn and delicata), as well as the standard orange Halloween jack-o'-lantern belong to this species. In its oldest form, rarely seen nowadays, C. pepo appears to have spread into the Southwest from Mexico around 1000 AD. It should also be noted that in the past there was no difference between summer and winter squashes. The latter were simply allowed to ripen fully to the stage most suitable for winter storage. Summer squash were simply immature squash eaten before seeds or a hard rind developed. Also of note is the pepo decorative gourd, inedible but seen in homes throughout the United States around Thanksgiving. These are not to be confused with the larger hard-shelled utilitarian gourd, also in the *Cucurbitaceae* family, the *Lagenaria siceraria,* raised for containers, rattles, and so forth.

C. moschata—This squash is believed to have arrived from the east some time after the pepo. Although there are many varieties still found in northern Mexico today, in U.S. commerce this species is represented mainly by the butternut and occasionally the long curved-neck Tahitian, which is extremely rich in sugars.

C. maxima—Native to the highlands in Peru, Bolivia, and Chile, maximas are believed to have been unknown in the Southwest before the Spaniards brought them northward. This is interesting upon considering that with few exceptions (mostly Navajo), C. maxima pumpkins—mostly very hard-shelled hubbard, turban, and cheese types—are currently raised primarily in the traditional Hispanic high-mountain villages of New Mexico.

C. argyrosperma (formerly *C. mixta)*—When native squash is discussed in the Southwest, this is the one mentioned ninety percent of the time. Varieties of this mostly pear-shaped, green and white striped pumpkin are found throughout the region and are considered as old as agriculture in the region. Also known as the *cushaw,* these are also raised in the Southeast where they are fed to livestock as much as or perhaps more than to humans. Although not typically as sweet as the other three species, the argyrosperma has more uses.

Dry and nutty or damp and sweet, flesh from all four species is edible, although in unimproved native varieties flavor can differ dramatically from one fruit to the next even when harvested from the same plant. Rich in proteins, carotene, and vitamin A, they are baked or roasted whole in hornos or coal pits. Entire squashes do keep exceptionally well, but small bruises or punctures can shorten storage life. Hence, squash was often sliced into rings or more commonly, continuous spirals, and hung to dry for winter stews.

All four species' seeds can also be shelled and eaten, containing 25 to 35 percent oil and up to 30 percent protein. In some places in Mexico, the seed is the more important part of the harvest than the flesh. Seeds are used raw or roasted for snacks, and ground into butters and eaten as is or mixed with chile, fruit, or other condiments as pipian mole.

Many Cucurbita varieties sacrifice quantity of flesh (and often flavor and edibility) for quantity of rich seed. The seeds of these varieties furnish twenty times the calories and twice the calcium of the flesh as well as higher rates of vitamins.

It is surmised that edible cucurbits were derived from some edible mutation of the hard-shelled gourd. Horribly bitter-fleshed, hard gourds were domesticated for their edible seeds and, before the advent of pottery, their shells. The gourds served for storage of foodstuffs, water, or whatever would fit into them. Although breakable, they are lightweight and easily transported. Once heavy, fragile pottery was developed and integrated into everyday life, movement among the people was curtailed and gourds became most important for lightweight canteens, or for rattles and ceremonial use.

I have yet to see a maxima or pepo shell used in these ways in the Southwest, but the argyrosperma is used. Left alone,

most other squashes will mold, rot, and collapse. With sufficient air circulation, an argyrosperma will dry to a shell that is
less sturdy than a *lagenaria* gourd, but is sound nonetheless.
These shells have been used for rattles or instruments, and were
presumably treated in the same manner. All utilitarian gourds
are boiled before use to harden them (but especially for dippers
and canteens to cleanse the shell of bitter, dry pulp still cling-
ing to the interior).

By the time pumpkins are cured for storage (when shells are
too hard to dent with the fingernail) and gourds set to dry (a
winter-long process), all crops have been harvested. Cool
weather brings deer and elk hunts for fresh meat or winter
jerky. Cattle, brought down from summer mountain pastures,
will be turned into the fields to clear the standing cornstalks
or frosted bean vines. Dry beans and chicos, ears of corn for
milling or posole, and even carefully handled melons—all
these are laid by for storage.

Wood is split and stacked. Nothing warms like a wood fire
and nothing, the elders will say, tastes so good as the old foods
cooked on its heat. It's time to gather 'round these fires, to turn
inward and renew, to hear the stories the old ones have to tell.

Seeds for next spring have been selected and reverently put
aside. It is not forgotten that each seed is alive, a gift from the
Creator but also held in trust for your grandchildren's grand-
children. Soon enough, the rest period of farming's cycle will
again give way to spring planting for human and spirit sus-
tenance. This echoing of the circles of life that spiral from the
ancestor toward the grandchild and back again is possible only
with the nourishing gifts the Creator has blessed upon the
people's existence.

NOTE

1. Worldwide, whole grain is looked upon as peasant food and rarely seen as desirable. In the rice-based cultures of Asia, for example, white rice is the civilized food to eat. An American friend of mine spending time in Korea had to journey to a mill to find whole-grain brown rice. The workers and customers were incredulous that he would even consider eating what was looked upon as hog feed.

REFERENCES

Andrews, Jean. *Peppers.* University of Texas, 1984.

Crosby, Alfred W. Jr. *The Columbian Exchange.* Greenwood Press, 1972.

Ebeling, Walter. *Handbook of Indian Foods and Fibers of Arid America.* University of California Press, 1986.

Foster, Nelson and Linda S. Cordell. *Chilies to Chocolate.* University of Arizona Press, 1992.

Fussel, Betty. *The Story of Corn.* Knopf, 1992.

Garcia, Fabian. *New Mexico Beans.* Las Cruces, New Mexico: New Mexico College of Agriculture Bulletin 105, 1917.

Glanzberg, Joel. *The Corn Is the Same as the People.* Santa Clara Pueblo, New Mexico: Tribal Agriculture Project, 1994.

Heiser, Charles B. *Seed to Civilization.* Harvard University Press, 1973.

Nabhan, Gary Paul. *Gathering the Desert.* University of Arizona Press, 1985.

Scheerens, J.C., A.M. Tinsley, I.R. Abbas, C.W. Weber, and J.W. Berry. "The Nutritional Significance of Tepary Bean Consumption." *Desert Plants* 5(1983). Arizona State Parks Board, Boyce Thompson Arboretum, Inc., and University of Arizona.

Wilson, Gilbert L. *Buffalo Bird Woman's Garden.* Rep. ed. University of Minnesota, 1917. Minnesota Historical Society, 1987.

Woodbury, Richard B. and Ezra B.W. Zubrow. "Agricultural Beginnings, 2000 BC–500 AD." *Handbook of North American Indians,* vol. 9, edited by Alfonso Ortiz. Smithsonian Institution, 1979.

3

"It Is Time to Plant"
The Real Green Revolution

Kenny Ausubel

Plowing field with alternating rows of corn and squash at Santa Ana Pueblo, New Mexico. Photograph © Marcia Keegan.

New Mexico has long been a crossroads of herbal knowledge. The Pueblo Indians, who date their history in the area back 40,000 years, hold an intimate connection with the land and plant life. When the Spanish arrived in the fifteenth century, they brought with them their own plants and practices. When the Anglos arrived from Europe in large numbers in the 1800s, they transported precious botanical allies. These traditions converged to form a rich and unique legacy, which has since served as a primary source of health and healing.

Even today, herbal medicine comprises the primary health care for about eighty percent of the world's population. About a quarter of modern pharmaceuticals are directly derived from plants, and fully half are modeled on plants. Botanical medicine is the cornerstone of modern pharmacology and, as we approach the end of the twentieth century, the global renaissance of herbal medicine is proving that nature is a far more sophisticated chemist than any state-of-the-art laboratory. At the heart of botanical medicine is the profound reservoir of Indigenous knowledge, gleaned from millennia of living in intimate relationship with the natural world. One biologist compared the loss of knowledge when a shaman dies to the burning of an entire library.

While attending the Anthropology Film Center in Santa Fe, New Mexico, in 1979, I made a short film with herbologist Michael Moore as he gathered and processed local herbs. The film was well received and I parlayed it into my first documentary, "Los Remedios: The Healing Herbs," depicting the cross-cultural botanical traditions of the Southwest.

Around the same time, my father died suddenly of cancer. Shortly after his premature death, I received an unsolicited newsletter in the mail containing testimonials of people maintaining they had been cured of cancer using nutritional means. I was skeptical, even hostile to the idea. Like most people at that time, I believed what the doctors told me, that is, cancer was largely incurable and treatable only by conventional methods of surgery, radiation, and chemotherapy. But with my father freshly buried, I decided that if there were any truth at all to these surprising testimonials, I had to know. I embarked on a journey of personal investigation, reading everything I could get my hands on, and talking to anyone who had direct experience.

The Hoxsey Legend

I soon encountered a lesser-known world of remarkable remissions of people who got well when they weren't supposed to. The stories were miraculous and they were legion. As the trail heated up, I came across the astonishing story of Harry Hoxsey, an ex-coal miner with an eighth grade education who had inherited his family's herbal cancer remedies.

According to the Hoxsey legend, his great grandfather, a Quaker horse farmer in southern Illinois, found his prize stallion with a malignant tumor on its right hock. He couldn't bear shooting the animal, so he put it out to pasture to die peacefully. Three weeks later, he noticed that the tumor had stabilized, and from that point he began to closely observe the horse. Hoxsey found the horse browsing in a particular area of the pasture containing a profusion of weeds, shrubs, and flowers, and eating unusual plants that were not part of its normal diet. Within three months, the horse was completely well, and John Hoxsey went into the barn where he began to experiment with different combinations of the plants. He added ingredients from other popular home remedies of the day and devised three formulas.

John Hoxsey became famous for treating animals with cancer and tumors, and he passed on the formulas to succeeding generations. His grandson was the first to try the remedies on people, reportedly with positive results. John's great-grandson, Harry Hoxsey, went on to establish the first Hoxsey Cancer Clinic in 1924. As his fame spread, he ran up against the newly powerful American Medical Association, precipitating a thirty-five-year pitched battle with organized medicine. Two federal courts upheld the therapeutic value of the treatment, while thousands of patients claimed the treatment cured them. Hoxsey gained the support of senators, congressmen, judges, and even some doctors.

Throughout the struggle, Hoxsey sought a fair scientific test of his medicines. But organized medicine adamantly blocked him, deriding Hoxsey's herbs as a "bunch of weeds" unworthy of investigation. Despite winning numerous battles, Hoxsey finally lost the cancer war. The herbal treatments were banned at the height of the McCarthy era, and the Hoxsey organization became the first alternative cancer clinic to flee south of the border to Tijuana, Mexico, where it has continued since under the direction of Hoxsey's chief nurse, Mildred Nelson.

I resolved to make a film about the Hoxsey story. I spent almost four years researching the dramatic saga, called "Hoxsey:

How Healing Becomes a Crime," unearthing a sleeping giant of a story. But I was amazed to learn that even in 1985, no one had ever looked into the medical properties of the Hoxsey herbs. I then tracked down James Duke, Ph.D., a world-renowned expert on medicinal plants, at the U.S. Department of Agriculture near Washington, D.C. Duke dialed into NAPR-ALERT, a global computer database of botanical medicine. He found some surprising data.

Duke said that almost all the Hoxsey herbs were ancient Native American herbs used in treating cancer for over 3,000 years. He also noted that traditional folk remedies such as Hoxsey's showed a seventy-five percent correlation with positive medical activity. In other words, when people have used herbal remedies over time in this way, the formulas are very likely to have genuine efficacy. Duke then found modern scientific studies under controlled laboratory conditions validating anti-cancer and anti-tumor activity for six of the nine Hoxsey herbs.

Duke also noted that during the lifetime of Hoxsey's great grandfather, Illinois was the western frontier of the United States, right on the edge of Indian country. He surmised that it was almost certain John Hoxsey had contact with the Indigenous people and likely learned some of his plant medicines from Native traditions, as well as from "horse sense."

Other research I uncovered corroborated the fact that animals such as Jane Goodall's chimpanzees have often been observed traveling far from their feeding grounds to nibble on plants with medicinal properties. The notion that human beings learned about the healing qualities of plants by trying each one themselves, in hopes that they would heal rather than poison, is generally preposterous. Indigenous peoples have long watched four-leggeds to glean what finely-tuned animal instinct has already discovered.

Seed Preservation and Biodiversity Gardens at San Juan Pueblo

While in Washington, D.C., I met another prominent botanical sleuth, Christopher Bird, co-author of the famous book, *The Secret Life of Plants.* Bird had been busy documenting the fact that, in controlled experiments, plants showed emotions, feelings, and perhaps even some form of consciousness. We became friendly and, several months later, Chris phoned me at home in Santa Fe with a request. A friend of his was creating an interesting garden in an Indian Pueblo near Santa Fe and wanted me to make a short film about the project. I agreed.

Cradled between the Jemez and Rocky Mountains, the Rio Grande valley is a timeless place, the traditional home of the Pueblo peoples. The Rio Grande is the main waterway traversing this arid desert region. The river brings fecundity to the land and has long supported a farming culture for the Pueblos. When Pueblo peoples speak of agriculture, they really mean "agri-culture," a rich legacy of a profound human interconnection with the land and its blessings of food plants. Throughout the year ceremonial dances and rituals celebrate the gifts of the Earth, giving thanks for corn, beans, seeds, rain, and the mysterious tapestry of sacred relationships that sustain human beings and all life.

I didn't know what to expect when I arrived at San Juan Pueblo, but it was not anything I could have anticipated. There I met a young hippie named Gabriel Howearth, an Anglo who also had Tarahumara Indian ancestry. Gabriel had been a student of Alan Chadwick in California, an inspired gardener who reinvented organic gardening and believed it to be a critical path to world peace. Chadwick told his students that if they really wanted to learn about organic gardening, they should apprentice with Indigenous peoples who have been doing it the longest and the best. Howearth headed south to Mexico where he studied with Mayan Indians and learned about gardening by the stars, using crystals for fertility and double digging for building soil. Double digging, a state-of-the-art technique that many contemporary organic gardeners use for aerating the soil to promote exceptional plant growth fertility, is actually an ancient Indigenous practice, not a modern discovery.

Howearth subsequently ventured further south into remote areas of Ecuador to learn from other Indigenous communities. As people came to trust him, they shared with him their most precious gifts: seeds. Many Indigenous peoples believe that the voices of the ancestors speak through seeds and that by planting the seeds, we become ancestors for succeeding generations in a sacred transmission.

Howearth began to collect these revered and often rare seeds, focusing mainly on traditional Indigenous food plants of the Americas. But many of these plants were rapidly disappearing or becoming extinct as people left the land in the late twentieth century. San Juan Pueblo hired Gabriel for exactly that reason. Since World War II, Pueblo farmers have been increasingly joining the wage economy and leaving the land because they cannot make a living farming. The Pueblo has had to face the tragic loss of its ancient agricultural traditions. Perhaps this young Anglo seedhead and master organic gardener could help revive those traditions.

Howearth planted his biodiversity gardens at San Juan Pueblo. I spent about three weeks there with him, filming and learning. His gardens contained numerous plants I had never seen. As an enthusiastic but admittedly novice organic gardener myself, this rich world was entirely new to me. He was growing amaranth, the sacred grain of the Aztec civilization, which formed a startling scarlet plume against the turquoise New Mexico sky. This abundant nutritious grain had once almost been exterminated by the Spanish conquistadores. Partly because of its blood-red color, the Spaniards believed it was part of Aztec blood sacrifice ceremonies and banned it. Recently the National Academy of Sciences documented amaranth as a crucial food in the struggle against world hunger because of its exceptional nutritional properties as well as its prolific production and adaptability. It is the most popular grain today in India, where its tasty green leaves are also a delicacy. Gabriel had a dozen dazzling varieties growing in a glorious bouquet of fragrance and color, making it easy to see why many gardeners also prize this plant as a striking ornamental.

Nearby he had planted multiple varieties of *quinoa,* the sacred grain of the Incan civilization. Each year the Incan emperor ceremonially planted the first quinoa with a golden spike. With a delicious nutty flavor, quinoa too has exceptional nutritional value and has also been highlighted by the National Academy of Sciences as an important world food grain. It contains amino acids complementary to those found in conventional wheat, rice, and corn.

Entire societies of tomatoes of every imaginable shape, size, and color were also nearby. There were rare herbs, multicolored corns, and a diversity of food plants that tasted as good as they looked. Upon biting into an ear of Mandan Red Corn, developed by the Mandan tribe of the northern plains of North Dakota, I tasted for the first time the corny flavor of real corn. It was nothing like the super-sweet ears of corn from the supermarket. This was real, substantial food—a hearty meal in itself —whose palpable vitality I could feel resonating in my body.

While creating this backyard biodiversity, Gabriel respectfully put the word out in the Pueblo community to see if anyone had any old seeds. Every few days he would find a small yellowed envelope or crumpled packet of seeds left on his doorstep.

One day, as I stood behind the cameraman filming, I watched the sun glint off the bright red corn seeds held gently in the upraised hand of a Native American farmer. He had unearthed these scarlet jewels in a little clay pot embedded in the mud wall of his adobe home. Showing them around the community, he found only a couple of elders who still remembered what they were. They marveled at the sacred red corn of San Juan Pueblo that no one had grown in forty years. Tears rose in the farmer's voice. This humble man planted the sacred seeds, and began harvesting a spiritual homecoming in his ancient tribal community near the Rocky Mountains of New Mexico.

In these seeds lived not only the genetic legacy of countless generations of Pueblo farmers, but also the imprint of their hands. These crinkly scarlet seeds glowed with the songs, prayers, and gritty growing secrets of all the farmers who had come before, a tenuous heritage that must be applied to be preserved. Their rediscovery would lead to a historic revival of Native agriculture at the Pueblo. In that farmer's hands, I saw the profound interconnectedness of human beings with the Earth. A slender thread binds the weave tight in the intricate, mysterious fabric of life, and yet we have been blindly unraveling the tapestry of creation. As we strain the limits of the natural world, we can no longer escape the knowledge that ecological collapse has been the often unrecognized force behind the downfall of many civilizations. Biology is indeed destiny.

These traditional seeds, I learned, were under serious threat of extinction worldwide. Modern agribusiness built an industry based on the use of a package of hybrid seeds and toxic chemicals. These hybrids, the cross of two parent strains that yield what is called a first-generation hybrid, are "mules" which do not reproduce at all, or do not reproduce true to form. Unlike traditional open-pollinated seeds, which freely multiply with the generosity of nature, these hybrids compel farmers to return every year to the company store. Giant corporations can patent the hybrids, claiming ownership of a type that makes it illegal for farmers and gardeners to trade seeds or save them for their own use as they have done for millennia.

Moreover, the hybrids are conditioned to grow within the narrow tolerances of petrochemical fertilizers and pesticides. Large petrochemical and pharmaceutical companies have systematically bought up seed companies in a torrent of "vertical integration" to control the food supply from seed to store shelves. One direct consequence of this monopolistic feeding frenzy is the throttling of diversity. Because traditional open-pollinated seeds cannot be patented, they are of little interest to agribusiness corporations.

This genetic erosion is a grave threat to the global food supply, since diversity is the heart of evolution. The only constant in nature is change, and open-pollinated varieties are the proven survivors of floods, droughts, plagues, insects, and all the vagaries of the unending dance of the natural world. These seeds represent the source of adaptation essential to survival in evolution. This humble garden at San Juan Pueblo represented the invaluable legacy of humanity's coevolution with food plants. In fact, about sixty percent of the world's food plants were developed by Native Americans. For instance, without the food plants of the Americas, there would be no Italian food as we know it. Tomatoes, peppers, potatoes, and chiles all come from Indigenous people of the Americas, not to mention chocolate, sugar, and tobacco.

Food plants are not "natural" in the sense of spontaneously occurring in their current forms in nature. Rather they have been bred, cultivated, refined, and conserved by countless generations of brilliant gardeners and farmers. This living treasure of humanity's collective heritage is now in the red zone of cascading extinctions. Just since the time of our great grandparents (around 1900) 97 of 100 such plants are no longer available. Biologically speaking, we are not playing with a full deck.

I thought I was at San Juan Pueblo to make a film, but it turned out I was there to start a seed company. I went on to cofound Seeds of Change, a mission-driven venture devoted to conserving the world's ark of agricultural seeds by commercializing them in a partnership with backyard gardeners.

Shortly after I cofounded the company in 1989 with Howearth, we had a seminal experience at the farm in Gila, New Mexico, where we grew many of the seeds. By some serendipitous synchronicity, a U.S. Department of Agriculture tour was routed to the farm. Among the visitors was Abdullah Ibrahim, Minister of Agriculture from Dakar, Senegal. Gabriel led the group on a tour, ending at his research garden where he had many unusual varieties. Gabriel suddenly noticed the African visitor weeping. Inquiring what was the matter, he learned that

Ibrahim was responding to the sight of the traditional sorghum of his region, seeing it for the first time since his grandmother planted it when he was a child. It had since been supplanted by the hybrid sorghum now used throughout Africa.

Restoring Native Food Plants and Cultural Heritage

Ibrahim asked whether we could bring him back to the farm to study traditional plants and gardening practices. At the time, we were a tiny, struggling company, and had no money for such a project. But deeply moved by his plight, I felt we needed to do something. I raised some additional funding from a sympathetic individual to start a nonprofit organization, later named the Collective Heritage Institute, to sponsor the Native Scholar Program to help conserve open-pollinated seed stocks and traditional farming practices.

Over the next few years, several Native American farmers attended the Native Scholar Program at the Gila farm. There was valuable exchange of information and knowledge, even though the program was minimally funded and we could not put the kind of energy and attention into it that it deserved. Among those who consulted on the project was Dr. Gregory Cajete, an educator from Santa Clara Pueblo who was especially knowledgeable about Native American food plants and farming traditions. He began work on creating a curriculum for schools that would convey the profound legacy of Native agriculture and food.

About the same time that I started the Native Scholar Program, I also founded the Bioneers Conference, an annual gathering of environmental visionaries with both feet on the ground. The Bioneers, a term I coined to describe biological pioneers using nature to heal nature, are innovators who have demonstrated viable models for environmental restoration. Their work spans many areas, from biodiversity conservation to bioremediation using natural treatment systems, to cultural, spiritual, and political strategies for repairing the damage we have visited upon the Earth. The Bioneers Conference has galvanized a budding, but disparate, culture around the "biological model" of interconnectedness. I saw that we needed to go beyond a human-centered Declaration of Independence to a biological Declaration of Interdependence. The time had come to unite nature, culture, and spirit in service of the restoration of Earth and our relationship to the web of life.

Prominent in the Bioneers network since its inception has been a very strong voice from the Indigenous community. Native peoples are the world's original bioneers, practicing a profound understanding of how human beings can live in a harmonious and respectful balance with the life of the world. Many representatives from Native communities have spoken at the Conference and the gathering has also served as a focal point to bring together individuals, groups, and companies working toward similar goals of restoration. The gathering has helped serve to launch initiatives and collaborations.

Increasingly, however, the word coming to us from Indian communities was that people were leaving the land because they couldn't make a living farming. Traditional knowledge, as well as seed stocks, were continuing to be marginalized and the pace was accelerating. What to do?

In 1994, I left Seeds of Change because of a difference of vision in the company's direction. (It was acquired shortly thereafter by candy giant M&M Mars Corporation.) Along with my partner and wife, Nina Simons, I retained management of the Collective Heritage Institute, where we are now able to focus more of our time and attention. We decided that the most productive course would be to adapt the Native Scholar Program into an economic development initiative based around family farming, including Native American growers as well as the larger universe of family farmers. Renamed the Restorative Development Initiative (RDI), the program seeks to create positive economic development based around "restorative" agriculture. The RDI acts to link Native American and other family farmers directly with progressive companies and markets to facilitate the creation of an alternative agricultural economy outside the commodities markets. The program also helps advance the use of restorative farming practices, which repair soil and water, as well as restore community-based economies.

The overarching problem is that corporate economic globalization is intensifying the centralization of capital. Agriculture, which is arguably the biggest business in the world, is also the single most environmentally destructive human activity. It is increasingly technology based and "unemploys" people at a dramatic rate. Farmers have become just another economic "input" in the agribusiness system. Multinational companies go where labor is cheapest and environmental regulations weakest. Farmers are vulnerable to rising and falling commodity prices, and may easily lose their land in a bad year. Even in a good year, they are barely surviving. As such, corporate agribusiness is causing large-scale ecological and social destruction. At stake is the control of the world food supply, the basis of national and tribal sovereignty.

Meanwhile, companies are themselves vulnerable to market

fluctuations. It is difficult to run a business where the supply of raw materials is variable, prices are unstable, and quality is uncertain. Progressive companies which seek to practice ecologically sound agriculture are penalized by this system. They too must compete with the ruthless global economics of commodities markets.

Restorative development seeks to remedy both economic and ecological conditions. As Paul Hawken (author of *The Ecology of Commerce*) once told me, sustainability is simply the midpoint between restoration and destruction. In light of the severe environmental degradation occurring worldwide, merely sustaining is not adequate—restoration is the goal.

Restoration is a broader concept which must include economics, jobs, ecology, biodiversity, nutrition, and community. The RDI acts as a facilitator to help family farms connect directly with progressive companies and markets. Unlike conventional farming, which is technology based, restorative agriculture is knowledge and labor intensive. As such, it holds the potential to create jobs and "unemploy" technology. Creating positive employment is one of the core virtues of restorative farming, which in turn restores community economies.

Each party has interests that can be well served by such a partnership. Farmers may gain a stable long-term relationship, as well as a "value added" for their product via restorative farming practices and specialty crops. Companies gain supply and price stability. Presumably, the quality of crops can be increased with restorative methods. All parties also gain important marketing advantages through promoting the positive social value of supporting restorative family farming.

In launching the RDI, we expanded our circle through collaborating with Sebia Hawkins (a former Greenpeace activist with a long-term relationship to Native American rights) to include several Native American leaders. Joining the team were John Mohawk, a Seneca from the Iroquois Six Nations who formerly edited the respected *Akwesasne Notes,* and who has been a farmer for twenty-five years; Oren Lyons, an Onondaga chief and global diplomat on behalf of Native rights; and Tonya Fritchener, founder of the American Indian Law Alliance. Both John and Oren also serve as professors of American Studies at the State University of New York at Buffalo. Another participant is Ralph Paige, an African American activist who founded the Federation of Southern Cooperatives, which represents the last 10,000 Black farmers in the United States and an equal number of poor white farmers, mostly in the Southeastern region.

Because of my involvement in founding Seeds of Change, I became part of the burgeoning community of socially responsible businesses. I came to know the founders and CEOs of numerous alternative companies that pursue the "double bottom line" of both profits and a social mission. Several of these companies are dedicated to environmental improvement and supporting ecological agriculture and family farms. I assembled a "founding circle of companies" committed to these goals, businesses willing to redirect their product sourcing to ecologically responsible and family farmers. A sampling of these companies follows: Odwalla, the Eclectic Institute herb company, Frontier Natural Products, East Earth herb company, Angelica Kitchen restaurant, Aubrey Organics cosmetic company, Earthrise Trading Company, and Real Goods, which markets sustainable energy products.

As the first part of this endeavor of linking farmers with markets, we assembled a national database of Native American farmers who wanted to participate in commercial farming.

Maggi Banner, a gifted filmmaker of Hopi-Tewa lineage who worked with the program for several years, contacted Native farmers around the country and collected the core of the database. Then we began assembling a shopping list of what the various companies want to purchase, along with prices and quantities. This process is currently underway.

The lead company in this venture was Odwalla, a producer of juices and nutritional beverages. Odwalla needed citrus at certain times of the year when it is not readily available from Florida. Maggi made connections with Indian growers in Arizona, whom we visited along with Arty Mangan, Odwalla's sourcing agent. Discussions are continuing with these parties in a long-term effort to establish positive commercial relationships. Arty has since joined the RDI as full-time project manager, bringing his unique skills of operating in the commercial market into alignment with his deep commitment to organic growers and family farmers.

In the process of contacting Native growers, we also discovered that many communities are producing one or several food products. Maggi assembled an array of these products and we launched a business plan to examine various scenarios for marketing these products more widely. This process is still underway, as we are exploring multiple innovative channels to distribute Native and family farm-based products for a better financial return to the growers.

Meanwhile, with John Mohawk we launched an initiative to develop traditional Iroquois white corn as a commercial product. We linked John with two prominent progressive restaurants, Angelica Kitchen in New York City, and the White Dog Café in Philadelphia. Leslie McEachern, owner of Angelica Kitchen, has a longstanding commitment to supporting strong relationships with local organic farmers. She and her chef Peter Berley joined John for a "tasting" on the Iroquois reservation where about forty-five people spent two days cooking together. They made entire meals featuring Iroquois white corn, from appetizers to entrées and desserts. Leslie and her chef helped advise John on what it would take to make these meals viable in a restaurant setting. We subsequently held a special cooking workshop at the Bioneers Conference.

John then spent Thanksgiving of 1997 at the White Dog Café assisting with the restaurant's Native Thanksgiving meal. He had the full support of owner Judy Wicks and chef Kevin Von Klaus, both of whom are also committed to using the restaurant to support organic farmers and social activism. He taught Native foods, cooking, and lore. The Iroquois white corn is reputed to be the corn that the Iroquois shared with George Washington's troops when they faced starvation at Valley Forge. It is among the most delicious and nutritious of sweet corns.

Several other nationally acclaimed chefs generously contributed recipes after experimenting with Iroquois white corn in their kitchens. Mollie Katzen, author of the famous *Moosewood Cookbook,* joined Deborah Madison, coauthor of the equally revered *Greens Cook Book,* in devising mouth-watering dishes which we again served up at the Bioneers Conference for food writers. The food fairly flew off the plates, including an elegant polenta, shrimp corncakes, and John and Yvonne Mohawk's traditional cornbread recipe. The bottom line is that, even in a blind taste test, this food has an exceptional flavor premium distinguishing it from any other corn, especially hybrid candycane junk. Putting aside the idea of a social mission for a moment, the food stands on its own formidable merits.

The idea behind these sorts of events is to promote a broader awareness and appreciation of Native foods and to create a demand for them. Restaurants and recipes by noted chefs help provide a cultural platform to draw interest and attention. In 1999, both Angelica Kitchen and White Dog Café placed sizable orders to use the corn in their restaurants, and other customers are also seriously interested. Mounting demand will secure an economic base to support the growers and restore biodiversity in the food supply. It also helps conserve endangered seed stocks by keeping them in active cultivation.

The corn project is expanding with help from First Nations Development Institute, a Native American financial development institute. The goal is to create one or more Native owned and operated businesses that support their communities. The project is now scaling up production to meet demand and building the necessary infrastructure to fulfill orders and market the products.

We are now exploring strategies for various foods and crops that will support farmers, restore food diversity, and provide added value for ecological farming practices. Apart from the fact that farmers can earn good income from specialty crops, there is also extra value in "branded agriculture," where the very methods of cultivation bring added value. Organic foods bring farmers a premium price, and the growth of the organic market has been steady—at present the U.S. organic food market totals about $4 billion per year. In Europe, biodynamically grown products also fetch higher prices and are much sought after. One idea we have explored is the possibility of creating a "Native Grown" certification for Indian farmers. Many consumers would place extra value on Native-grown foods. The herbal market is another arena experiencing tremendous growth.

The use of medicinal herbs has now entered the mainstream, evidenced by the fact that herbs are readily found in most drugstores and supermarkets. In Germany, sales of medicinal herbs have surpassed $3 billion a year, and in the United States, around $4 billion per annum. While this phenomenon of more people turning to natural medicine would seem to be a good thing, it also presents certain problems. Many herbs are now "wildcrafted," or gathered from natural landscapes; as demand has increased, these plant populations are being depleted, and in some cases, devastated. Consequently, a shift to cultivation of these herbs is essential, which means that many more skilled growers are necessary. Moreover, because these plants are medicines, the value of organic cultivation takes on an added importance.

The organic herb sector represents a major growth opportunity for farmers. We started an herb growing project with African American farmers in the Southeastern United States, who are in dire need of alternative economic strategies to stay on the land farming. Of the 10,000 such growers still left, only about 200 are under the age of sixty-five, and finding specialty crops and new markets is a matter of survival. The Eclectic Institute herb company under the direction of founder Ed Alstat is committed to purchasing organic herbs from these growers, and we have conducted training sessions to get the process going. The first crop is expected in 1999.

In 1997, John Mohawk, Oren Lyons, Sebia Hawkins, and I visited Mildred Nelson, the courageous nurse who has operated the Hoxsey Bio-Medical Center in Tijuana, Mexico, since 1963. We visited at length and discussed the possibility of employing Native American growers to cultivate the Hoxsey herbs. Since these plants have a long history of Indigenous usage, producing larger quantities of high quality herbs while supporting Native American growers could be a viable strategy. There are many other opportunities in the herbal cultivation area as well. In 1996, I brought some other colleagues to visit Mildred, including Oren Lyons and John Mohawk. As professors of American Studies at the State University of New York at Buffalo, both live in the dual worlds of traditional Indigenous culture and post-modern mainstream society. They came because they were deeply concerned about a close friend dying of a brain tumor. They were also intrigued with the Hoxsey herbal treatments whose origins owe much to traditional Native American plant lore.

Mildred believed her mother was part Indian, having grown up in the Oklahoma Territory in Indian country. Oren and John talked about how young people today no longer go down to the riverbed where the herbs grow, and how volumes of the rich Native heritage of botanical knowledge are vanishing in a single generation. Oren described the Indigenous view of herbs, which are considered to be sacred plants whose permission must first be asked before they can be used. He observed that Native peoples have generally not grown medicinal herbs, but wildcrafted them in the natural settings where they concentrate their special power.

Both John and Oren expressed interest in cultivating the Hoxsey herbs on the reservation, where today there is a small but meaningful rebirth of traditional herbalism, and where cancer is epidemic. Oren spoke slowly, with the same idling pauses that punctuated Mildred's languid storytelling. From a traditional perspective, he said, it is the spirit that heals, though the herbs and the medicines help.

Mildred was captivated by the conversation about plants,

animals, traditional culture, and, always, cancer. She was having increasing difficulty obtaining high quality herbs, which for many years were supplied mainly by Mormon, Amish, and Mennonite growers who farmed without chemicals. But their children were losing touch with the land as well, and the botanical future looked unstable. The movement of Native Americans out of farming in the past thirty to forty years, of course, means that knowledge is being lost and young farmers are scarce.

Consequently, another crucial facet of the RDI is a program to help train growers, especially young people, in ecological farming practices that will allow them to produce crops of exceptional quality exceeding rigorous commercial sourcing standards, while also introducing unusual varieties. We are setting up a network of "lighthouse growers" to supply this training. These lighthouse growers offer their own farms as working models of restorative agriculture, and some of them are willing to travel to visit farmers on site to address their locale-specific conditions.

In 1998, we inaugurated these lighthouse grower trainings, which were very positively received. Two workshops featured Native American growers. During one trip, members of the Native American Farmers Association traveled to the Arizona farm of Native Seeds/SEARCH to study traditional Indigenous seeds and cultivation methods. Another group journeyed to California to visit four top sites there, including medium and large commercial farms, as well as a very successful community-supported agriculture project servicing its own area with diverse crops of ultra-high quality.

Federation growers visited several farms in the Southeast that use innovative practices and produce specialty herbs and other crops. The RDI program is also developing marketing assistance, because communicating the authentic story of traditional plants and growing practices is important, both to sell the products and to preserve Native Americans' cultural heritage. John Mohawk and Gregory Cajete are participating with Indian communities in an effort to ensure that their story is elegantly told. We are working in a similar way with the Federation of Southern Cooperatives and the growers it represents.

Another issue faced by Indigenous growers is intellectual property rights. Although a highly controversial area, these rights must somehow be addressed to halt or prevent exploitation. After blue corn became a hot item in the marketplace, its Indian origins were exploited without respect in the marketing frenzy of companies capitalizing on high customer demand. Many companies used the names of tribes such as the Hopi as if they no longer existed. No compensation of any kind was awarded to the tribes and, of equal importance, the cultural heritage of blue corn was misrepresented.

The American Indian Law Alliance is working with the RDI to ensure that Indigenous rights are protected. Inevitably, as products become popular, greed and envy set in, and ultimately it will be a challenge to prevent unscrupulous businesses from exploiting the popularity of products of Indigenous origin. For this reason it may become essential to use a Native American-grown certification, similar to the certification that has been developed for Indigenous arts and crafts.

Since I first visited San Juan Pueblo in 1985 and witnessed the return of the sacred red corn, the community has revived its ancient farming tradition and built a modern food processing facility. In a culture where "food is life," restoring of "agri-culture" is both a material and a spiritual act. Those humble corn seeds reignited a 40,000-year-old farming legacy that the Pueblo hopes will carry it successfully into the next century, reestablishing the ecological balance between the tribe and the Earth in a sacred partnership.

During a Collective Heritage Institute meeting about the RDI, Oren Lyons suggested that life can be like crossing a river. Once you have stepped onto a stone, only then can you see where the next step lies. We are proceeding one step at a time now and will undoubtedly look back to see some missteps. While it is imperative to speak the truth and criticize the corporate system of agribusiness, it is also essential to envision and create the alternative economy that will support farmers and the land for the generations to come.

Unless we ourselves create this alternative farming future, it simply will not be there for us in 2010. Oren Lyons shared with us a current Iroquois prophecy that crystallizes the situation. The vision says, "It is time to plant."

REFERENCES

Ausubel, Kenny. "Hoxsey: How Healing Becomes A Crime." Film produced by Realidad Productions, 1987.

_____. "Restoring the Earth: Visionary Solutions from the Bioneers." Film produced by HJ Kramer, 1997.

_____. *Seeds of Change: The Living Treasure.* HarperCollins, 1995.

Hawken, Paul. *The Ecology of Commerce: A Declaration of Sustainability.* HarperBusiness, 1994.

Katzen, Mollie. *The Moosewood Cookbook.* Ten Speed Press, 1992.

Madison, Deborah and Edward Espe Brown. *The Greens Cook Book.* Bantam, 1987.

Tompkins, Peter and Christopher O. Bird. *The Secret Life of Plants.* HarperCollins, 1989.

For information on the Collective Heritage Institute, the Bioneers Conference, and the Restorative Development Initiative, see the Web site, www.bioneers.org, call 1-877-BIONEER or 505-986-0366, or write 826 Camino del Monte Rey, A-6, Santa Fe, NM 87501.

4

Indigenous Foods, Indigenous Health
A Pueblo Perspective

Gregory Cajete

Corn, bean, and squash seeds displayed on a metate *(grinding stone).*
Photograph © Brett Bakker, Native Seeds/SEARCH.

Historical Perspective

Human evolution has been intimately intertwined with the use of available animal and plant food sources. Hunting and gathering adaptations, followed by the development of agriculture, required the full application of human intelligence, cooperation, and social developments such as the extended family, language, and various forms of practical education and environmental awareness. It was hunting and gathering that led humans to migrate to the far reaches of the earth. During this stage of human history, hunting of big game marked the most pronounced development of human exploitation of a variety of animals and plants used as food.

Inherent in this evolutionary development was a high level of nutritional diversity and relative health. From a historical perspective, Characin and Whitney (in Ebeling 1986:6) state that "just as aboriginal peoples uniformly lack heart disease, are of high physical activity, low psychological stress, and low cholesterol intake, so also they lack malocclusion because their diets are high in chewing stress and low in carbohydrates."

The transition from hunting and gathering to agriculture by some aboriginal peoples also led to new nutritional and health challenges. Aboriginal peoples who remained largely flesh eaters generally tended to have less tooth decay, degenerative diseases, and intestinal dysfunctions than those eating a mixed diet. The incidence of these diseases increased as this mixed diet became more "civilized" and replete with refined sugar and other highly processed foods.

The relationship of diet to degenerative diseases among aboriginal peoples has been extensively researched. For example, Leon Abrams (1980) found that "Eskimos still living on their traditional diet of land animals, fish and birds...enjoyed excellent health...[T]hey obtained vitamin C by eating the adrenal glands of the animals they hunted...[I]n addition they suffered low incidence of coronary atherosclerosis and acute myocardial infarction due to the large levels of eicosatetraenoic acid (good cholesterol) in the marine animals which they traditionally consumed."

In contrast, Schiffer (1972) points out that "When Eskimos adopted the white man's diet, which consists largely of refined carbohydrates such as white flour and sugar, processed polyunsaturated fats and other processed foods, they became widely afflicted with all degenerative diseases of our modern society" (quoted in Ebeling 1986:7).

Similar effects have been documented for every aboriginal population that has been colonized or has otherwise assimilated the modern Western diet. Indeed, change of diet remains the single most identifiable factor in degenerative health situations throughout the world. It is particularly significant as an acute degenerative factor among aboriginal populations.

Acute degeneration, of course, was not always the case. For instance, "At the time when Columbus discovered America, the Indians were using two thousand different foods derived from plants, a figure Europe could hardly have matched" (Oboimsawin 1980:26). Indeed, at the time of Columbus's first voyage, the Indigenous peoples of the Americas were among the healthiest in the world. Within the first fifty years of contact with Spanish colonizers, many Indian populations were devastated as a result of new diseases and disruption of their lives. The effects of European-introduced diseases notwithstanding, American Indigenous peoples overall continued to display enormous vitality and health well into modern times. Much of this vitality was a direct result of their diverse and nutritious diets.

Nutritionally related diseases were commonplace in Europe in the 1500s and 1600s, but nearly nonexistent in pre-Columbian America. Vitamin deficiency was common in Europe, while in America the Native peoples were eating extensive and various quantities of green pot herbs in every form. Green salads of such plants as salmonberry, coltsfoot, fiddlehead fern, wild celery, and wild onion were common. Green leafy pot herbs were also common in soups and stews, and flowers such as those of squash, wild nasturtium, and sunflower were commonly used.

Similar dietary diversity was common among the pre-Columbian Pueblo populations. Indeed, Pueblo uses of plants for food, medicine, and other adaptations reflect an amazing versatility that was characteristic of all Amerindian peoples. The story of Pueblo foods is an extension of the evolution of Indigenous peoples on the American continent. As big game began to dwindle, Native peoples increasingly depended upon smaller animals and plants. Gradually, food preparation and domestication of plants gave rise to sophisticated forms of agriculture. This evolution took particular forms among the ancestors of today's Pueblo peoples.

The foods of Indian America formed the foundation of their historic pre-Columbian health. How then did such diversity of foods evolve in Indian America? In order to answer such a question and understand it within the context of Pueblo foods, agriculture, and diet, it is important to reflect on the following broad themes of influence. These include the themes of food development in America and the development of Native cuisines that characterized the various tribal traditions. Each of these themes when woven together form a tapestry reflecting how extensive and ancient the traditional diets of the Pueblo and other tribes are and coincidentally why the drastic changes in Indigenous diets over the span of just a few generations have had equally drastic impacts on the health of Indigenous people.

Food Development in America

Every American Indian tribe has a long history of relationship with plants in their respective environments. It is probable that Indians of the Andes did more experiments with plants than any other people in the world. There is speculation that Macchu Picchu was not only an Andean ceremonial center but an agricultural experimentation center as well. Macchu Picchu is surrounded by terraced gardens of every shape and orientation where the Inca planted and experimented with plant varieties. They attempted to develop strains of plants adapted to every type of soil and climatic condition. The potato or *papa* was the most commonly "experimented" plant, but was by no means the only one. The enormous diversity of potatoes, numerous strains of maize, amaranth, quinoa, and dozens of other plants evolved from thousands of years of experimentation by Andean peoples.

Incan experimentation is but one of many documented examples of Indian agricultural science. Every Indian tribe conducted long-term experiments with plants, animals, minerals, and other natural characteristics of their environments. Yet underneath all such experimentation was a set of guiding principles based on establishing and maintaining a sacred relationship that formed the foundation of healing, health, and wholeness in Indian societies. The perception of food as sacred, with certain foods being designated as symbolic to the life and well-being of a tribe, was and continues to be a guiding principle in traditional societies around the world. Animal source foods, followed by gathered or planted foods, have been venerated by traditional societies through ritual and ceremony. Indeed, it may be said that the first ceremonies and rituals revolved around life-sustaining foods recognized by paleo-Indigenous societies.

The foundations of sacred and life-sustaining foods are also intimately tied to emotional, physical, and spiritual health, which constitute the understanding and expression of wholeness in an Indigenous society. It is this complex interplay of relationship, diet, sacred food, and concepts of health and wholeness that formed the vital dynamic of traditional diets and helped create the level of health achieved by Indigenous societies (Schmid 1997:xii).

Studies of Traditional Culture Diets

One of the most comprehensive works on traditional foods and their effects on health is that of Dr. Weston Price, a dentist who became interested in the relative lack of tooth decay and other dental abnormalities in isolated Indigenous populations. For Price, the general state of teeth and the existence of dental decay are good indicators of a patient's general health. He also suspected that the health of a patient's teeth was directly related to nutrition. He had noticed in his extensive practice of dentistry over many years that there was a significant change for the worse in dental health of the children he had as patients in contrast to their parents. Price undertook a study that carried him to every corner of the earth in search of answers to the dramatic change he had witnessed in the deterioration of the dental health of his adult patients' children. A change that essentially had taken only one generation needed to be understood in its broadest and most elemental context. He believed that some of the answers might be found among Indigenous populations who still relied on traditional diets or who only recently had adopted modern foods such as refined sugar, white flour, canned foods, and vegetable oils.

Price's study encompassed members of communities of the high alpine Swiss; Gaels of the Outer Hebrides; Alaskan Eskimos; Native communities throughout Canada and the Western United States; Hawaiians, Melanesians and Polynesians; Aborigines in Australia; Maori in New Zealand; Eastern and Central Africans; Malaysians; and Indians of the Peruvian Andes. Since Price's studies took place in the 1930s he was able to capture the last remnants of Indigenous societies still subsisting on traditional foods.

Through Price's study and several that have followed, a portrait of the effects of dietary change in traditional societies has become clearer. While the various effects of adopting the modern diet are complex, multidimensional, and unique to the special circumstances of individuals and communities, the deterioration of relative health is obvious. Traditional wisdom and foods are the largest single factors in protecting traditional hunter-gatherer-fishing societies from dental decay and chronic disease (Schmid 1997:8).

In situations where there was a dramatic shift in the relative health of the Indigenous populations Price studied, adoption of the modern diet was clearly the single most substantial cause. He called this phenomenon "intercepted heredity," referring to the interception of a hereditary pattern of exceptional dental health by poor diet. It is clear from Price's studies that once Indigenous people lost certain understandings of fundamental nutritional laws and living in harmony with their environments, their health declined dramatically (Schmid 1997:22).

Such understandings included detailed information about using specific parts of animals and the unique importance of each part, as well as the medicinal uses of herbs. When this accumulated wisdom was not passed on to the next generation or ignored, the results were sickness, death, and degeneration of succeeding generations (Schmid 1997:17). It is the traditional wisdom of Indigenous societies that "prescribed specified kinds and quantities of foods known to ensure fertility, the birth of healthy, perfectly formed babies, and optimal development of growing children" (Schmid 1997:13).

Selected insights gleaned from Price's studies among traditional societies are summarized below.

▲ The "quality" of food mattered, especially in terms of the ability of various foods to fortify individuals against chronic illness. That the quality of food mattered, in terms of its ability to nourish and maintain the life and health of a community, was a well-developed concept in traditional societies. The principal foods of each Indigenous group were also the most nutritious, and therefore were considered sacred and celebrated in ritual, ceremony, art, and story.

♠ Each of the groups Price studied had developed a special combination of meat, fish, grains, fruits, vegetables, and gathered plants that worked best for them in their respective environments.

♠ In comparing the relative dental health of each group studied, it was obvious that groups maintaining traditional diets lacked tooth decay. When a particular group adopted modern diets, major deterioration of their dental health occurred, usually within one generation.

♠ Price found many traditional food regimes to contain quantities of organ meats such as adrenal glands (Vitamin C), eyes (Vitamin A), livers (Vitamin D and iron), and kidneys and hearts (also high in iron).

♠ Invariably Price found that the meat eating herdsmen-hunter-gatherer-fisher peoples were typically healthier, stronger, and consistently better off nutritionally than agriculturalists. Next, communities that maintained their traditional agriculture were in far better relative health than city dwellers subsisting on a modern diet of refined foods. "Wherever Natives had used large amounts of refined foods for some time, decay was rampant and tuberculosis prevalent; other chronic diseases appeared in time. The Natives' immunity to infectious diseases typically striking foreigners disappeared; they too became susceptible. Dental arch abnormalities commonly appeared in the next generation" (Schmid 1997:21).

♠ In many cases traditional Indigenous foods were eaten raw or only slightly cooked. This was true of fish, organ meats, fats, and varieties of plants used by traditional societies as food. Raw and slightly cooked foods retain most of their original nutritional qualities. This was particularly noticed by many traditional societies and gave rise to the notion of eating certain traditional foods raw as a means of preventing certain diseases, ensuring fertility, and promoting the growth of children.

♠ The ceremony and ritual surrounding the eating of sacred foods and the social context of sharing food through communal feasting were founded on a complex of traditional ideals that might be described as "building right relationship" to one's food and sources of life. The fact that most, if not all, traditional Indigenous ceremonies involve feasting, sharing, and exchange of food reflects the depth of common ideals of sharing, reciprocity, community, and relationship to all life expressed in traditions surrounding Indigenous foods. In the final analysis, "food is life," and this central truth of human existence was a guiding paradigm for behavior and relationships among traditional peoples.

These seven areas of general insights gained from Price's studies among traditional peoples around the world attest to the essential importance of traditional foods to Indigenous peoples. Studies have also shown that Natives from traditional societies who had adopted modern diets and suffered degenerative diseases, showed remarkable recovery rates upon returning to their traditional diets. An example of this phenomenon occurred among the Tohono O'odham (Papago) and revolved around dietary intervention as a treatment for adult onset diabetes (Nabhan 1985).

Historical research of traditional diets reflects that high protein diets of meat and fish were the preferred foods, with many examples of these foods being designated as sacred and central to the spiritual and physical well-being of a tribe. Hunter-gatherers were without equal in their ability to efficiently use the plant and animal food sources in their environments. It is therefore not surprising that they developed both an intimate relationship with and knowledge of their environments. Traditions, rituals, and mysticism revolving around the hunting, gathering, and sharing of animal foods served to reinforce and perpetuate both the intimate relationship and knowledge of these ancient and traditional sources of life.

Hunter-gatherer diets contained as much as ten times the fiber as that of modern diets. Calcium from plant and animal sources was two to three times as high, while sodium intake was only one-sixth that of today. Protein intake was twice as high. Hunter-gatherer diets also contained much less vegetable and saturated animal fat and significantly more polyunsaturated animal fat than modern diets (Schmid 1997:52). Given all of this historical evidence of dietary adaptation, it is little wonder that Indigenous populations who have made a dramatic shift to modern dietary habits suffer degenerative health effects such as heart disease, diabetes, and obesity within only one or two generations.

Pueblo Farming

Pueblos created their communities around the activity of farming. Soil and water availability in Pueblo territory varied. Given these environmental challenges, Pueblo people became masterful farmers and evolved numerous and effective strategies for farming.

Pueblo farmers ranged far and wide in search of potential farming possibilities. Their first choices were the mesa tops, which had become covered with windblown deposits of reddish soils (loess). The mesas of the southwestern United States became the first sites of full-scale food production by the Pueblos. There are no rivers or perennial streams; in most canyons water runs only following heavy summer thunderstorms or intermittently during the spring snow melt. Annual precipitation varies from 14 to 18 inches (350 to 450 mm), with most of it coming as snow between January and March. This winter precipitation is important for vegetation. There are also reasonably dependable summer rains from mid-July through August. Many small springs and seeps provide drinking water. The frost-free growing season is reasonably long (161 to 170 days) and there are moderately hot summer temperatures for crop growth (Ebeling 1986:548).

The early Pueblo farmers were highly successful in the application of dryland farming techniques even when cycles of drought, common in these mesa lands, would occur. Such application was accomplished through the use of multiple, strategically placed garden plots and the construction of many check dams and terraced plots. This practice resulted in silt collection in small washes and canyon bottoms that could then be planted in a short crop cycle to provide foodstuffs even in the driest seasons. These early Pueblo farmers were experts at anticipating runoff water and working with the unique characteristics of southwestern mesa lands. Later Pueblo farmers (1300–1600) practiced irrigation farming as Pueblo populations began to move to more adequate water sources along the Rio Grande after the "great drought" that occurred during the 1200s.

Farming, traditional foods, pottery, basketry, and community are all highly interrelated aspects of Pueblo history, life, and tradition. The acts of gathering, growing, preparing, and storing food are at the core of Pueblo community life, health, and well-being. This highly complex relationship to food, combined with its deep cultural meaning, informed the spirit and practice of Pueblo farming. "The spirit of farming and connection to nature in our Native communities is disappearing with the modern ways of farming. One does not realize the value of the land and crops. Farming used to be done by families who were involved with nature. It was good to get your hands all muddy and dirty, to feel and smell the earth. We knew which areas were good for planting vegetable gardens and where to plant wheat, corn, and alfalfa" (Martinez 1997).

There has always been a special relationship between Pueblo people and their gardens. Pueblos cared for their gardens as they would care for their family and community. Their gardens received such attention because they were literally the foundation for the life and well-being of family and community. In tending and nurturing gardens, Pueblos also nurtured their own lives, the essential lesson of Pueblo gardening. Although much has been lost, Pueblo people still continue to garden and remember the importance of gardening as a way to come to know what is important in life, individually and communally.

Plants such as corn, beans, and squash have been given a special place in Pueblo Indian traditions. Stories of the origin of corn are connected to the origin of the Pueblo people themselves. As has been stated many times, for Pueblo people corn is a metaphoric symbol for human life, relationship to nature, and the expression of a deeply embedded sense of caring for life. Farming traditions are still strong in some Pueblo communities. In others, traditions lie dormant as the result of the interplay of historical, economic, and sociocultural factors whose cumulative effect has been to disconnect an entire generation of Pueblo people from their gardening roots, traditional foods, and healthy nutrition.

A natural place to begin the regeneration of the Pueblo gardening tradition is through the creation of Pueblo teaching gardens. A natural inclination on the part of many young Pueblo people is to bring forward their best qualities when gardening or just being in nature. The garden becomes not only a place to watch plants grow, but a direct way for young people to participate in the greater circle of life. As young people work the soil, plant seeds, nurture seedlings, and harvest crops, they experience the fuller development of their natural connections and participate in the age-old Pueblo way of connecting to place and living a healthy life.

Pueblo Foods: An Enduring Tradition

Traditional uses of plants and animals by Pueblo peoples present at once a unique and highly representative case study of Indigenous dietary forms. Pueblos today represent all stages of Indigenous use of plants and animals extending from the paleo-Indian hunters of 8,000 to 15,000 years ago through the hunter-gatherer phase, and then through the agricultural phase to the present phase of transition to modern dietary habits. The Pueblo story of traditional foods also represents the dilemma of the forces of cultural assimilation and cultural preservation working simultaneously in the modern context of Pueblo communities. The Pueblos have adapted the foods of many traditions into the context of Pueblo life through a selective process that has categorized foods as traditional, Spanish, and American. These categories are very much related to the historical introduction of these foods to Pueblo communities.

Traditional foods have long been a central form of the Pueblo peoples' life and tradition. Pueblo foods connect Pueblo people to their land and community, and to a hunting-gathering and agricultural way of life that has sustained them through millennia of relationship in the Southwest. Only within the last few generations has this "way" of traditional food use begun to give way to significant changes. As is true of other Indigenous peoples, with these significant changes in food and lifestyle the incidence of diet-related illness and all inherent social consequences have increased.

Traditional Pueblo foods are not only a matter of tradition and a source of survival, they are also a sacrament and in and of themselves a representation of the sacred. Symbolic foods such as corn have a central place in Pueblo traditions. "Corn is who we are"—a phrase used by some Pueblo elders—captures the sentiment and relationship of the people to corn. As another Pueblo elder relates, "Ever since our emergence from the underworld, corn has had a very special meaning to Pueblo people. We use it in our ceremonies. We use it to live; we use it to feed our animals; we start with it; we end up with it. We give thanks to our creator for its existence" (Dasheno 1994).

In Pueblo tradition, corn is a symbolic representation of a whole complex of agricultural and gathered foods that have been a part of Pueblo adaptation to the Southwestern environment. The Pueblo symbolization of corn along with that of deer, elk, buffalo, and other wild game represents the twofold foundation of traditional subsistence on plant and animal life. This primal relationship to plants and animals is celebrated in Pueblo planting, harvesting, and rain-bringing dances associated with corn, and in various animal dances, which are performed in conjunction with the yearly cycle of the ceremonial calendar. Such activities commemorate these essential Pueblo relationships in ways that perpetuate key understandings about the use and preservation of these life-sustaining foods.

In ancient times the plant and animal foods used by Pueblo ancestors included almost everything edible in the Southwestern environment, as revealed by excavations at various Paleo-Indian, archaic, and basketmaker sites. Bat Cave excavations in the Mogollon region of southwestern New Mexico reveal 61 species of plants and over 1,600 identifiable animal bones. In addition to early forms of corn, gathered plants included varieties of grasses and seeds, prickly pear cacti, yucca, and piñon. Large animal bones included those of mountain sheep, deer, pronghorn, antelope, and elk. The bones of small animals found include kangaroo rats, pocket mice, dog, wolf, coyote, rabbits, porcupine, badger, woodrat, and pocket gopher, to name only a few.

Bat Cave findings are reflective of what has been termed the "Lakeshore Ecology Phase," dating from 8,000 to 10,000 years ago at the beginning of the transition of Southwest Indian populations from hunter-gatherer cultures to agriculturalists. Bat Cave is exemplary of settlements established by glacial lakes at the end of the last ice age. These ancient lakes provided fish, aquatic insects, and varieties of edible plants as food sources for Indian populations of the period as well as excellent soil for planting. It is estimated that well over 600 species of plants, animals, and insects may have been used by Southwestern Indian groups in this area alone (Ebeling 1986:456, 461).

A list of the most common wild plants used by Pueblo peoples would include piñon, juniper berries, cattail, mesquite, Indian rice grass, sedge, wild onion, sego lily, agave, yucca, cottonwood, mulberry, juniper, mistletoe, wild rhubarb, goosefat, salt bush, amaranth, pokeweed, chickweed, purslane, barberry, desert plume, pepper grass, watercress, Rocky Mountain beeplant, tansy mustard, gooseberry, currant, wild rose hips, thimbleberry, chokecherry, service berry, catclaw, milk vetch, desert mallow, canyon grape, bee balm, puccoon, dog bane, milkweed, snakeweed, buffalo gourd, plantain, devil's claw, wild potato, cut leaf nightshade, green thread, sunflower, rabbit brush, sagebrush, prickly lettuce, marsh elder, and chicory. This list is by no means exhaustive, but is representative of the diversity of wild edible plants consistently gathered by Pueblo peoples. Gathered plants such as these combined with varieties of cultivated corn, beans, squash, and, later on, chiles form the foundation of traditional plant foods.

Traditional Pueblo foods also form the foundation for the distinct physiology that evolved among the people as a result of their adaptation to this unique diet. Indeed, Indigenous peoples' physiology and physical characteristics were largely a subset of the nutritional characteristics of their diets. The historic differences in physical appearance between Indigenous groups residing in different regions and subsisting on different diets were quite apparent. This is to say that there was a characteristic Pueblo physique distinct from a Lakota physique, which in turn was distinct from a Tlingit or Iroquois physique.

Historically, Pueblos tended to be small to medium in size, sinewy, small-muscled, and small-boned. The Pueblo physique contrasted with that of the Plains Lakota who tended to be tall, long-muscled, and long-boned, as is typical of aboriginal herdsmen around the world. The point here is that nutrition influences the physiques of Indian people, and body types varied from region to region based largely on traditional food types. As both the Pueblo and Lakota peoples transitioned to modern diets, their characteristic physiques also began to change. This process continues among contemporary Pueblo children.

While changes in physical characteristics can be observed and recorded, physiological changes on the other hand are more difficult to track and are noticed only after they become symptomatic. Current tendencies of Pueblo people toward diabetes, heart disease, and obesity may, in this context, be said to be symptomatic.

Biologically, desert and semi-desert peoples have adapted to feast and famine cycles characteristic of desert ecologies. It is logical to assume that the physiology of desert and semi-desert peoples evolved to meet the challenges of their environments. When their lifestyles change dramatically, so does their relative health. "NIH (National Institute of Health) researchers have long postulated that a developed 'thrifty gene' may be at work, a genetic change that allowed the first inhabitants of North America to adapt to 'feast or famine' conditions before European colonization. According to this theory, the availability of water and food was inconsistent and led Native Americans to store food in extra fat cells for later use...[S]toring calories as fat enabled the tribes to survive famines, resulting in increased insulin secretion. Developed over centuries, this pattern has resulted in a high level of obesity among Indians today, because of high glucose levels and ineffective use of insulin" (Higgins 1991).

The above excerpt refers to recent studies carried out among the Pima. Like the Pima/Papago peoples of Arizona, the Pueblo peoples of New Mexico and Arizona share not only a predisposition to diabetes, but similar cultural and political challenges such as marginalization and poverty that contribute to reliance on the modern "poor man's diet" staples that are typically highly processed, and filled with salt/sugar. The transition from the traditional to the modern (poor man's) diet and lifestyle provides the context for the dramatic change in Pueblo health. This transition has a history that must be understood if real and sustained progress is to be made in addressing health problems such as diabetes. How did Pueblos and other tribes come to adopt the "poor man's diet"? For contemporary Pueblos, how can they once again have the opportunity to revitalize traditional diets as a part of their everyday lives?

Foods, Dietary Choices, and Nutritional Education in Pueblo Communities

Food is central to Pueblo communal thought and traditions. Traditionally, every aspect of the gathering, cultivation, and sharing of food is steeped in ritual and meaning. In earlier days, everyone in Pueblo communities was intimately tied to securing food in some form. As such, food figured in every important traditional education process in Pueblo communities. For instance, young would-be farmers were traditionally taught in formal and informal ways everything they needed to know about planting corn and other traditional Pueblo food staples such as squash, beans, pumpkin, melons, and chiles. Young Pueblo women were traditionally taught all aspects of food preparation from grinding corn to baking bread to preparing varieties of meats and stews. This metaphoric and practical relationship to food in turn extended to Pueblo art forms, dance, music, land use and tenure, social organization, and world view. Pueblo pottery, for instance, is imbued with symbolic meaning from its very conception, through its production, and into its use as a utilitarian container of food. The meaning of pottery as a container of life connected to the sacredness of food is a traditional expression of Pueblo understanding of relationship to the sources of life. "Corn is who we are," therefore, has a literal as well as metaphoric meaning in Pueblo history and tradition.

Corn, beans, squash, and chiles in their various forms combined with gathered foods and wild meats comprised the traditional pre-Columbian Pueblo diet. With the coming of the Spanish in the last half of the sixteenth century, extensive additions were made to this foundational diet. Being agriculturalists, the Pueblos accepted many new foods and plants appropriate to Pueblo tastes and the environmental conditions of their homelands. Pueblos learned to eat beef, mutton, chicken, pork, and various fruits such as apples, pears, and grapes. They also learned to grow and use various new crops (e.g., wheat) and herbs (e.g., anise). Yet in spite of newly introduced foods, Pueblos continued to rely on their traditional cultivated foods as staples.

When the Santa Fe Trail was opened in the early 1800s, new foods such as coffee, cane sugar, and rock salt were introduced to Pueblos for the first time. This was the beginning of the Pueblo transition to the Western diet. But even this was a gradual process, largely based on the availability of "American foods." Pueblos remained essentially an agricultural society using traditional foods until the late 1920s when the railroads arrived in New Mexico. Change accelerated after World War II as many Pueblo men returned from the military after assimilating many American ways and American foods. After the war, there was added economic pressure to become more wage-work oriented as opposed to being solely or largely agriculture based. This economic trend had a direct effect on Pueblo agricultural lifestyles.

Over the course of only two generations Pueblo communities moved from self-sustaining agricultural economies to wage-based economies. The Pueblo generations after World War II adopted wage work as the predominant means of subsistence. Economics has enormous influence, not only on lifestyle but also "food style." As Pueblo people increased their intake of processed foods, the incidence of degenerative diseases also increased in direct proportion. Beginning with tuberculosis and then evolving to include heart disease, stomach disorders, obesity, diabetes, and cancer, the portrait of Pueblo health since the early 1920s has been dismal.

Changes in lifestyle and diet among the Pueblo mirror similar changes within other Indigenous groups. The move from the physicality of farming to the sedentary nature of most wage work, combined with the "poor man's diet" and the "ethno stress" of attempting to live in two worlds, are certainly all interrelated factors contributing to the relatively poor state of Pueblo health today. Education at various levels is a key to reversing the deterioration. Educating people already afflicted is of course an obvious area of focus. However, chronic illness such as diabetes evolves over time and the best cure is prevention. An educational emphasis on prevention necessarily begins with awareness of food nutrients and links to disease. Learning to create meals low in sugar, salt, and fat, implementing exercise programs, and community awareness are also helpful.

However, all such educational interventions fall short if the factors of revitalizing traditional diets and an understanding of physiological adaptation are not given serious consideration. The revitalization of Indigenous gardens and sustainable gathering of wild foods, especially those which have protective qualities with regard to diabetes, must also be encouraged.

Ultimately, the choice is that of the Pueblo people themselves. By deciding to recover their original diets, lifestyle, traditions of gardening, and adopting new and more healthy nutritional habits, Pueblo people can recover from the degenerative diseases of the modern "poor man's diet." Such recovery will require a form of health education that is culturally specific based on the revitalization of Pueblo wisdom regarding traditional diet and concepts of health and wholeness. This process can occur first by introducing Pueblo youth to their own "food history." This introduction necessarily begins within Pueblo communities themselves and then extends to include appropriate historical and dietary education as a part of Pueblo children's school curricula.

Next, Pueblo communities must consider the reintroduction or enhancement of Pueblo farming at a "communal" level in ways that each community deems appropriate. This reemphasis on communal farming creates a context in which important understandings and orientations may be shared and practiced. Finally, it is important for Pueblo communities, and the schools that serve their children, to find ways to collaborate in the education of Pueblo children as it relates to health and nutrition.

The Pueblo people's relationship to traditional foods embodies the very essence of Pueblo philosophy and ecological ethics. Pueblo people must respond anew to the perennial question of "what is education for" from their own unique frames of reference. Their collective answer to this ancient question carries with it consequences that are more profound now than they have ever been in Pueblo history. There is an old Pueblo saying that is often evoked when these types of crucial questions are posed. Variably translated, the saying simply relates that it is time to go to "that place the people talk about." This is not only a physical place, but also a place of consciousness. It is a place of soul and natural orientation.

REFERENCES

Abrams, H. Leon, Jr. "Vegetarianism: An anthropological/nutritional evaluation." *Journal of Applied Nutrition* 12(1980):53–81.

Dasheno, Walter. In Reyna Greene, "Corn Is Who We Are: Pueblo Indian Foods." Video. Smithsonian Institution, National Museum of American History, 1994.

Ebeling, Walter. *Handbook of Indian Foods and Fibers of Arid America.* University of California Press, 1986.

Higgins, Michael. "Native Peoples Take On Diabetes." *East/West Magazine* (April 1991).

Martinez, Esther. "Esther Martinez of San Juan Pueblo." In Gregory Cajete, ed., *Growing the Memories: Native American Farming,* pp. 32–36. Pojoaque Pueblo, New Mexico: Poeh Cultural Center, 1997.

Nabhan, Gary Paul. *Gathering the Desert.* University of Arizona, 1985.

Oboimsawin, Ray. "Traditional Indian health and nutrition." *Akwesasne Notes* 26(1980).

Price, Weston A. *Nutrition and Physical Degeneration.* Keats Publishing Inc., 1989.

Schiffer, Michael B. "Cultural laws and the reconstruction of past lifeways." *The Kiva* 37(1972):149–157.

Schmid, Ronald F. *Traditional Foods Are Your Best Medicine.* Healing Arts Press, 1997.

Weatherford, Jack. *Indian Givers.* Fawcett Columbine, 1988.

5

Traditional Diet and Health in Northwest Mexico

Enrique Salmón

Rarámuri Pascola (Easter) Dance, celebrating renewal of the land and life, in Norogachi, Chihuahua state, Mexico. Photograph © Enrique Salmón.

He came up from behind me so quietly and without warning that I was startled. My new walking companion smiled and said, *"Cuira,"* a Rarámuri greeting. I returned his greeting with *"Cuira-ba,"* and we quickly walked along the sandy arroyo bottom towards the village. Along the way we exchanged names, and he discovered from where I was walking and what I was doing in his mountains. Although I spoke his language, he surmised that I was from El Norte. Nevertheless, in a few minutes he asked if I liked to drink *tesguino,* a beer made of corn. When I said yes, his smile grew.

To the Rarámuri tesguino is more than simply an alcoholic beverage. It is a ceremonial sacrament as well as a nutritional supplement. All Rarámuri partake of tesguino from birth, when it is used to bless newborns, until their final days. Later in life it is consumed at all ceremonies and gatherings. Through consumption of tesguino, Rarámuri add to the strength of the Creator and ensure the survival of all life. When my walking companion determined that I drank tesguino he was assuring himself that I was a good Rarámuri.

Food, drinks, diet—the things that comprise the nutrition of an Indigenous culture—afford one of the most straightforward understandings of Indigenous life. A culture's diet reveals whether the people adhere to tradition or are assimilating into the larger culture. Assimilation induces Indigenous people to give up the "old ways" for the modern, and nutritious traditional foods are replaced by fast and alien foods. These new foods contain less nutritional value than the old foods, but hold greater social value. This transition has spelled near disaster for some Indigenous communities in the American Southwest where diabetes, obesity, heart disease, and even cancer are the high prices people pay for their new diet of Western foods (Eaton 1988).

In Northwest Mexico most Indigenous peoples have experienced some degree of assimilation into Mexican culture. Settlement by European descendants was slower here than in most of the United States. The result was a less dramatic assimilation of Indigenous people into Spanish and Mexican culture and thus, the foreign diet. Today Indigenous traditional nutrition in Northwest Mexico is little different from when the first Europeans arrived in the region during the sixteenth century. Most people continue to eat the staples of corn, beans, and squash supplemented with wild edible greens and other gathered foods. And even where assimilation has occurred, the foodways have not been greatly altered because the Mexican diet is based in large part on Indigenous staple foods. Consequently, the incidence of nutritionally influenced diseases is lower than in the U.S. Southwest. Still, modern fast foods have found their way into the region and the diets of Indigenous peoples, although to a much lesser extent.

This chapter examines the traditional foods of Northwest Mexico and their effect on the health of the region's Indigenous people. The pre-Columbian diet is compared to today's changing diets, followed by a survey of the nutritional benefits of a traditional diet. The intent is to explain why Indigenous people in Northwest Mexico, some only miles away from their relatives across the U.S. border to the north, suffer less from nutrition-related diseases.

Northwest Mexico: A Region of Cultural, Geographic, and Biological Diversity

Northwest Mexico is home to numerous Indigenous groups. After the Navajo, the Rarámuri are the second most numerous group of Indigenous people in North America. The Rarámuri occupy the high mountain ranges and deep *barrancas* (gorges or canyons) of the Sierra Madre in southwest Chihuahua. Their mountains are home to the Barranca de Cobre, a canyon deeper and larger than the Grand Canyon of Arizona. They speak an Uto-Aztecan language, which is one of the largest linguistic families in the Greater Southwest.

To the west in the desert thornscrub of northern Sinaloa and Sonora live the Yaqui and Mayo. These are the same Yaqui whose relatives, looking to escape genocide at the hands of the Mexican military, migrated north into Arizona at the turn of the century. They are closely related to the Mayo, who speak virtually the same language, which is part of the Uto-Aztecan family as well (Spicer 1940, 1954).

To the south and east of the Rarámuri stretching into Durango live the Tepehuan. In many ways they resemble their linguistic cousins, the Rarámuri. Their religious customs as well as their ranching-based lifestyles are similar to those of the Rarámuri. The Tepehuan are, however, more assimilated into Mexican culture. Most of the men and women wear Western clothing, compared to the Rarámuri where traditional, colorful attire is more common (Pennington 1969). To the west of the Rarámuri and still in the mountains live the Guarijio (Gentry 1963). They too are linguistically related to the Rarámuri. Like the Tepehuan they share religious and lifestyle practices with the Rarámuri.

In the arid hills and mountains of northeast Sonora live the Pima Bajo. Across the border to the north live their linguistic relatives, the Pima and Tohono O'odham. Culturally the Pima Bajo resemble their Indigenous neighbors in Mexico. They raise livestock and continue to follow religious customs that are a syncretic mix of pre-Columbian and Catholic practices (LeFerriére 1994:102). In the vicinity live the Opata. At one time the Opata followed a traditional lifestyle similar to that of the Pima Bajo. But later they voluntarily assimilated into the larger Spanish and later Mexican culture as a way to develop alliances against Apache raids. Opata bloodlines remain strong in the area but a distinct Opata culture has all but vanished (Johnson 1950).

Although the Mexican northwest region is home to several Indigenous peoples, the most numerous and culturally dominant group of people are the mestizos. Mestizo culture is Mexico: the cosmic fusion of Spanish, Indigenous, Moorish, Scottish, German, and French genes and influences form a vibrant culture that celebrates a European and Indigenous blend of customs and knowledge. Indigenous words embellish daily conversation as do Indigenous foods, which provide flavor and spice to Mexican cuisine. Mexican and Indigenous cuisine mirror the diversity attainable by people who are still knowledgeable about available foods.

Northwest Mexico is both geographically and biologically diverse. The Sierra Madre Occidental, a barrier on the eastern side, is a continuous range of montane woodlands originating in the Mexican states of Zacatecas and Aguas Calientes, and reaching north into the southwestern United States. From the western flank of the mountains and descending to the Sea of Cortez are the Pacific Tropical Lowlands which biologically represent the northern reaches of the Tropic Zone of the Western Hemisphere. The northern area of the region is bounded by the Sonoran and Chihuahuan deserts. The deep canyons, tall mountains, and high deserts all add to the region's isolation and slower pace of assimilation into Western culture. The Western Sierra Madre mountains, extending south from Arizona into Mexico and running parallel along the Sea of Cortez, are characterized by deep and narrow barrancas that were cut and gouged by the many rivers that drain the area. Some barrancas descend as deep as 3,000 feet, often providing two distinct ecological regions and habitats: highlands and gorges. Several varieties of hardwood and softwood trees are found in the woods of the cool highlands, whereas tropical flora characterizes the interior walls and floors of the canyons.

The transitional highland areas are drained by several rivers that run west from the Sierra Madre, including the upper Sonora, Mayo, Fuerte, and Yaqui rivers (Johnson 1950). The birds of the region caught the attention of Jesuit missionary Pérez de Ribas, who noted the varieties of parrots, macaws, turkeys, eagles, and woodpeckers that inhabited the forests. He also marveled at the bears, lions, jaguars, and wolves that stalked the mountains, canyons, and plains (Pérez de Ribas 1968).

The forests of the upper elevations feature fig trees, liana, pines, bursera, cassia, and several epiphytes. The forests are occupied by white-tailed deer, coati, boa constrictors, and ocelots along with numerous bird species. The thornscrub region is characterized by ocotillo, acacias, brazilwood, organ pipe, cardon cacti, and several other thorny, multi-trunked trees and shrubs (Brown 1994).

The gorges are so deep that a distinct change from alpine to tropical flora is noticeable as one descends. The giant agave, sotol, and cacti still exist on the canyon walls, but different species of trees and shrubs are found at lower levels, including the fragrant laurel tree and brazilwood. Several shrubs common to the gorges include the physic nut, cotton plant, wild tobacco, and indigo (Bennett and Zingg 1935).

Pre-Columbian Yoeme and Mayo took advantage of the fertile basins and rich alluvial plains for their farms located along the main waterways in Sinaloa and Sonora. A number of modern farmers still maintain small plots along the same waterways. Most of the region is thickly covered with brush and short-thorn deciduous forest comprised of mesquite, palo blanco, various cacti, saltbush, sage, agaves, and ironwood. Along the rivers cottonwoods and willows are found. Two rainy seasons feed the region. One arrives during the winter and the other in the summer. Winter flooding in the mountains makes spring planting possible on unirrigated land, and summer rains are sufficient for summer crops (Beals 1943). In the eighteenth century Jesuit priest Ignaz Pfefferkorn stated that "Sonora is altogether a blessed country. Sometimes, however, one travels eight or ten hours without finding a drop of water, a condition which is extremely inconvenient in such a hot country" (Pfefferkorn 1989).

The rugged nature of the landscape has been a major factor in the differing degrees of cultural assimilation. Pérez de Ribas described the mountainous area as being of "extreme height, and profound depth, altogether the most spectacular of all the Occidental Indies, if not the entire New World." He marveled that any Native peoples could penetrate the extremeness of the mountains and noted that the snows of the mountains reached the depth of sixty-six inches (Pérez de Ribas 1968).

The nature of the geography of northwest Mexico is one of rich dynamic variation. The complex geography, topography, and elevational changes result in the astounding amount of biodiversity in the region. At least eight "physiognomic vegetation types" can be found, including montane evergreen forest, oak-coniferous woodland, tropical deciduous forest, oak savanna, chaparral, short-grass prairie, subtropical thornscrub, and subtropical desert fringe (Felger and Dahl 1994). Northwestern Mexico houses the third largest concentration of biodiversity in the world (Brown 1994, Felger and Dahl 1994, Ramamoorthy et al. 1993). It is estimated that 4,000 vascular plant species—plants with vascular systems—are found in the region. Of the approximately 4,000, 150 are endemic, that is, found only in northwestern Mexico. In the Rarámuri region of the central Sierra Tarahumara alone, as many as 1,900 plant species can be found (Felger and Dahl 1994).

The region is home to eighteen important pre-Columbian food crops including domesticated agaves, pepperweed, panic grass, and tepary beans, in addition to endemic squash and maize species. Wild relatives of domesticated plants also occur in the area, such as wild species of agave, gourds, beans, chokecherries, and nightshades (Felger and Dahl 1994).

It is no accident that this region is biologically diverse. The Indigenous inhabitants have managed this region for at least 2,000 years (Harbottle and Weigand 1992:78, Nelson 1995:597, Nelson and Anyon 1996, Zingg 1940). Around 400 different plant species are used by the people of the region for food and medicine. However, mestizo populations in the area recognize and use only about forty percent of those used by the Indigenous people (Salmón 1995:44). These numbers reflect the strong reciprocal relationship the Indigenous inhabitants have maintained with their environment.

There is a link between cultural and biological diversity.

Jesusita and her grandchild, Carolina, collect edible greens in the hills and arroyos near their Rarámuri *ranchería* in the Sierra Madre of Chihuahua, Mexico. Collecting edible plants is not considered a chore. The practice of gathering plants reflects their relationship with the place that has always sustained them. The land offers edible mustard greens, chenopods, amaranths, and many other edible plants. Jesusita and Carolina often take time to stop their work to throw rocks into a stream and to laugh at their play and each other. Sixty years of often hard living disappear from Jesusita's deeply-lined and darkened face when she plays with Carolina. But Carolina is not only learning how to play; she is mastering centuries of accumulated knowledge that will help her, and many other children like her, to learn which greens to collect and when to collect them, as well as traditional land management that will ensure the survival of the plants.

Many surviving Indigenous cultures have inhabited and managed particular places for countless generations. Those who have held onto their languages have been more successful. This is due to the sophisticated ecological knowledge encoded in languages (Nabhan 1997, Salmón 1997). In Mexico economic and population crises are beginning to erode the remaining Indigenous languages and traditions. In turn, many traditional diets are being traded for processed foods offered by Western culture.

Cultures on the Edge of Change

In the United States the loss of traditional diets has been underway for several generations (Jackson 1994:381, Justice 1994:69). The most profound changes occur among the young who are raised in a "Big Gulp" nutritional culture. A significant portion of the Navajo daily diet, for example, includes fried processed foods, fast food meals, and carbonated drinks, all low in fiber and complex carbohydrates, and high in fat (Wolfe 1994:435).

In northwestern Mexico a "Big Gulp" culture has not yet emerged due to the absence of convenience stores, fast food restaurants, and ease of access to processed foods. Still, traditional foods, perceived by many Indigenous people as markers of low socioeconomic status, are being gradually replaced by elements of mestizo diets. Today *tortillas de trigo* (white flour tortillas) are preferred over corn tortillas. Most of the rural trading posts ship in and sell bottled cola drinks, candies, cookies, and chips. The degree to which these foods are included in the diet varies among the peoples of the region due to different degrees of availability and affordability.

Limited access to processed foods is part of the reason why Indigenous people in northwest Mexico may suffer less from diseases such as diabetes and obesity. In northwestern Mexico one rarely sees an overweight mestizo or Indigenous person. This is directly due to the differences in lifestyles here compared to those of the same types of people north of the border. Most people in northwestern Mexico continue to live a rural existence and, because most do not own cars, exercise is a function of daily living. They walk to tend their fields, and typically harvest and plow without engine-powered machinery. Collecting firewood is a rigorous chore. Women and children walk great distances to gather wild foods and craft-related plants. People will walk several miles just to visit relatives and friends. The children, who usually run, travel several miles in a day while playing. Without cars, access to processed foods is limited, while the daily exercise regimen helps them to maintain their weight and health.

It is indisputable that traditional diet and lifestyle are linked to optimum health in northwestern Mexico. When Western foods displace traditional foods and sedentary lifestyles replace active ones, general health deteriorates. For centuries the Indigenous peoples of northwestern Mexico satisfied subsistence needs with a large variety of domesticated and wild plants. These foods, along with the continuation of their active lifestyles, will be the keys to maintaining their health in the future.

The Future Is in the Past: Pre-Columbian Foods of Northwest Mexico

Northwestern Mexico has always been a region of abundance. Pre-Columbian granaries were stocked with many varieties of corn, panic grass, amaranth, chenopods, and beans. Squash provided ample supplements to meals along with domesticated and wild greens. In addition, seasonal foods such as cactus fruits, mushrooms, chiles, mesquite, yucca, and piñon nuts furnished periodic delicacies to the Indigenous palate (Minnis 1991:231). During the early decades of the sixteenth century Spanish explorers and conquistadores noted the abundance of the region and relied on Indigenous foods to feed their expeditions (Nentvig 1980, Pérez de Ribas 1968, Pfefferkorn 1989). To different degrees all these foods continue to be grown, collected, and consumed by Indigenous people in northwestern Mexico.

Corn (maize, *Zea mays*) remains the staple for most Indigenous peoples in the region and for mestizo populations as well. It is grown in small family plots, in one-acre fields, on forty-five-degree sloping milpas, along water courses, and in large-scale agribusiness farms. There are as many varieties of corn as there are cultures, habitats, and climates in northwest Mexico. The people of the region eat and drink corn in several ways. It is made into tortillas, which are eaten alone or folded into *tacos, enchiladas,* or *tostadas.* A dough made of corn and filled with chile and meat, and then steamed inside corn husks becomes *tamales.* Many travelers carry pre-fried *gorditas,* a corn dough formed into a circle, stuffed with any variety of filling, covered with another circle and fried into a type of turnover. Some travelers still carry *pinole,* roasted and ground meal. It is eaten usually with water and sometimes a sweetener. The mother of the family I often stay with in Chihuahua makes the most delicious corn and anise cookies. A mid-day snack often consists of melted cheese sandwiched between two corn tortillas flavored with salsa and lime. A unique method of eating corn is found in the consumption of corn beer. It is primarily the Rarámuri who continue this practice, but some Guarijio, Pima Bajo, and Tepehuanes consume the beer as well.

In order for the Rarámuri to honor Onorúame (the Creator) for his gifts of life, rain, and food, they prepare and consume their traditional corn beer, known as *batari-ki* in Rarámuri and tesguino in Spanish. Due to the effort involved in its preparation, tesguino is usually consumed only during the special corn beer festivals, called *tesguinadas,* which are an integral part of most Rarámuri community events, including religious festivals, ceremonial dances, and curing rituals. Dried corn kernels are sprouted and ground into a paste, which is then boiled in water for up to a day. Wild oat grass is sometimes added to the mixture, which ferments in large *ollas* (pots) until the day of the event (Salmón 1991:34).

During the tesguinadas, the Rarámuri consume large quantities of batari-ki. More than simply an alcoholic beverage, batari-ki is a sacrament used to communicate with the spirit realm. Batari-ki is also used as a sacramental blessing for the sick, newborns, farm animals, and fields. When it is time to pray for the fields and animals, or when Onorúame is sick or in need of nourishment, an *owéruame* (shaman/healer) will be instructed to conduct a special curing ceremony. The ceremony begins with the shaman making offerings of food and batari-ki to the four directions and to Onorúame.

The sacramental use of batari-ki is an important link in a chain of events that can never be broken. Without corn batari-ki cannot be produced, and without batari-ki Onorúame will die, the rains will stop, and the corn will not grow. A symbiotic cycle exists that cannot be halted. The Rarámuri need corn, and in a reciprocal fashion, the corn needs the Rarámuri. In essence, this is the central theme of traditional Rarámuri life as well as that of other Indigenous peoples in northwestern Mexico (Salmón 1991).

After corn, beans (frijoles, *Phaseolus spp.*) are the most important food item in traditional and modern northwest Mexican diets. Beans are often grown alongside maize in the smaller family and community fields. Many bean varieties are Native to the region. Pinto beans *(P. vulgaris)* are the most common species of cultivated bean in the region. Hundreds of bean varieties are still grown in the sierra to the desert lowlands, from lima *(P. lanatus)*, scarlet runner *(P. coccineus)*, and chubby bordales, to the intriguing chivitas.

The most successfully adapted bean to the area is the tepary *(P. acutfolius)*. Teparies are suited to the arid regions of Sonora where temperatures often surpass 105° F for several hours during the day. The small white, brown, and tan beans grow in pods on small bushes that require a minimum of moisture to grow and reach maturity. In fact, bean production decreases with overirrigation (Nabhan 1985). Crops of squash and pumpkins were important pre-Columbian foods and remain so today. Cushaws *(Cucurbita mixta* and *C. argyrosperma)*, warty squash *(C. moschata)*, blushers *(C. maxima)*, and pumpkins *(C. pepo)* continue to be harvested by Indigenous peoples throughout the region (Heiser 1985:57, Smith et al. 1994:407). If squash are not eaten fresh, the fruit is thinly sliced and dried to be used later in various dishes. Melons *(C. melo)* were introduced by the Spaniards and were quickly adopted by the Indigenous people of northwest Mexico. Both the muskmelon and watermelon became favorite varieties.

Wild foods are important supplements to the Indigenous diet. They are seasonal, often providing sources of food when domesticated plants are unavailable. Greens probably comprise the largest category of wild foods. Various types and species of lambsquarters *(Chenopodium spp.)*, amaranths, and pigweeds *(Amaranthus spp.)*, mustards *(Brassica spp.)*, plantain *(Plantago spp.)*, among others, are collected throughout the year.

Throughout the cool summers in the Sierra Madre, groups of colorfully dressed Rarámuri, Tepehuan, Guarijio, and Pima Bajo women and children can be seen slowly walking through open fields carrying plastic and paper bags. Every several steps they stop, bend over, and reach for the hidden green delicacies. The greens are eaten fresh or dried for later use (Bye 1981:109 and 1979:237, Smith 1994:407). One of my favorite recipes calls for dried pigweed fried with chiles and wild onions. Eaten with beans and corn tortillas these wild foods provide a traditional, healthy meal.

When I was young I would help my grandmother and mother collect *nopalitos* (prickly pear pads). Grandmother would hand me a paper bag and a long kitchen knife and tell me which prickly pear bush was ready. I would leave with final instructions for the maximum size of the pads to collect. I gathered the small, thin pads. With the long knife I was careful to keep the spines from my hands. Afterwards I would enjoy the fruits of my labor with some of Grandmother's prickly pear soup. I looked forward to the early summer when I would be asked to gather *tunas,* the juicy purplish prickly pear fruits. My mother and grandmother often cooked up syrups, candies, and jams from these seasonal gifts.

Prickly pear (nopalitos and tunas; *Opuntia spp.)* are found throughout the region and have been consumed by all people of the area. One of the more popular species *(O. phaeacantha)* is prized for its juicy fruits. But the pads and fruits of several species of prickly pear and other opuntias such as cholla are also used.

If the Indigenous peoples of northwestern Mexico had only to rely on the foods mentioned above, their diets would be limited yet still nutritious. Fortunately, many other wild foods are available. Wild chiles *(Capsicum spp.)* spice up the meals throughout the region. Acorns continue to be harvested in the foothills of the Sierra Madre and other mountainous regions. Mesquite pods are ground and eaten by Piman and other peoples. Wild onions and mushrooms are delicacies for the Rarámuri and Tepehuan. Saguaro fruits are gathered annually for the rain ceremonies by the Pima.

In the past, the Indigenous diet was largely vegetarian

(Beiner 1991:5). Animal protein was a small part of the diet, consisting of deer, javalina, wild fowl, rabbit, and other wild game. The first diet change arrived with the Spaniards, who introduced wheat, millet, and livestock such as sheep and cattle. But the regional diet continued to be based on whole foods with maize, beans, and squash as the staples, until the 1960s when modern foods began to replace many traditional staples. It is not unusual to see an elderly Rarámuri, draped in traditional clothing, strolling away from his mountain community drinking from a bottle of Coca Cola. Sweetened carbonated drinks, candy bars, and fat-laden snacks of both Mexican and American brands are sold by traveling vendors and from the small shops that dot even the most remote areas. But these items are luxuries for Indigenous peoples in the region. They have not replaced nor have they become a large proportion of the traditional diet. However, change has occurred in the products used in preparing traditional foods, such as a shift to animal fats which increase the fat and cholesterol content of once low-fat foods.

The degree of assimilation is directly correlated to the proportion of modern foods found in Indigenous diets in northwestern Mexico. For example, the diet of the least assimilated Rarámuri, who are isolated from large mestizo towns, is not greatly different from that of 300 years ago. However, people who live on the tourist trail and near mestizo towns consume less of their traditional diet and more modern high-fat, low-fiber foods. The Opata of Sonora are the most assimilated group in the region and consume largely a mestizo diet. The diets of the Tepehuan, Yaqui, Mayo, Guarijio, and Pima Bajo are comprised of both traditional and mestizo foods. Fortunately, the typical mestizo diet resembles that of the traditional Indigenous diet. Corn tortillas and beans are the staples. These foods are augmented with rice, wheat tortillas, chile, red meat, pork, and sometimes seafood. Compared to Indigenous diets north of the border, the mestizo diet is relatively low in fat and high in fiber.

Benefits of the Indigenous Diet

A North American hiker and writer traveling through the mountains and canyons of the Sierra Madre once asked a Rarámuri what the secret was of his people's endurance and good health. The Rarámuri went home and returned with a bag full of his secret high-endurance ingredients. In the bag were corn tortillas, beans, and squash (Fayhee 1987).

The benefits of the Indigenous traditional diet are numerous. Not only does the diet offer fuel for high levels of physical endurance, but it provides the ingredients toward the prevention of illness and disease. In brief, the traditional diet is high in fiber and complex carbohydrates, low in fat and cholesterol, and offers the full range of minerals, vitamins, and proteins required for human health. The soluble and insoluble fibers, complex carbohydrates, and mucilages help to control glucose and insulin levels, help people to avoid obesity, and lower cholesterol levels. As a result, the incidence of diabetes is very low among the Indigenous populations in northwestern Mexico. Obesity and heart disease are equally rare. Cancer and ulcers are virtually unheard of for people who subsist primarily on traditional foods.

People who are prone to or who already suffer from Type II diabetes need to regulate their glucose and insulin levels (Cowen 1990:350). Many traditional foods help to prevent and even solve this problem. Many modern processed foods contain little fiber and large quantities of simple carbohydrates. These foods are quickly digested, resulting in the rapid release of glucose and insulin. Fat accumulates along with a rise in blood sugar. As this process continues over the years, it can result in Type II diabetes (Brody 1991).

Traditional foods are slow to digest. Foods such as prickly pear, mesquite, beans, flour corn, wild greens and berries, acorns, and wild grains are all high in soluble and insoluble fibers and mucilages which prevent the body from quickly digesting carbohydrates and turning them into sugars. In addition, many of these foods contain a starch called amylose, which the body slowly digests resulting in the slow release of glucose and insulin. Starches found in modern foods such as white bread and potatoes break down quickly and precipitate high blood sugar levels that can trigger diabetes (Cowen 1990:350).

A study sponsored by the American Society for Clinical Nutrition tested the *in vivo* glycemic index of traditional foods (an index that reveals the speed at which certain foods cause the release of glucose and insulin). The test demonstrated that flour corn, mesquite pods, tepary beans, and acorns were all low in glycemic response and insulin release, ranging from 16 for acorns to 40 for flour corn. The glycemic index for canned sweet corn is around 59, while the index levels for other modern foods are much higher. The study demonstrated the importance of not only traditional foods, but also foods high in fiber and that contain slow digesting starches (Brand 1990:416).

Another health problem that strikes Indigenous people who turn to a modern diet is weight gain. Obesity is closely associated with diabetes and other health problems. The consumption of high-fiber traditional foods prevents obesity. High-fiber foods are low in fat and slow to digest, which helps to control the appetite. High fiber lowers serum insulin which also decreases food intake because insulin stimulates hunger (Anderson 1990:1488).

Today in northwest Mexico many young Indigenous men leave their communities to find temporary work elsewhere in logging operations, and on ranches and construction crews. Since they are working to make and save money they often live a spartan existence while on the job. To save money they consume lots of beans, because they are inexpensive, easy to cook, and taste good. Unknowingly, these young men are maintaining good health and preventing illness.

Beans are an especially important part of the traditional diet. Leguminous fiber found in beans has a special effect on postprandial (after-meal) glucose levels. It is the sudden rise in postprandial glucose levels that affects diabetes. After meals, glucose levels generally rise due to the digestion of carbohydrates and starches which transform into sugars. Eating lots of fiber in a meal can control postprandial glucose levels, but leguminous fibers seem to control glucose levels without having to stuff oneself with other fibers (Simpson et al. 1981:1). The mucilaginous bean coats slow down the digestion process. Beans are also high in proteins and complex carbohydrates, an additional nutrition bonus.

Another benefit of eating traditional unprocessed foods is the trace of chromium in the hulls and seed coats of grains and beans. Chromium deficiency has been found to cause insulin resistance. When foods are processed, the chromium in the seed coats and hulls literally goes down the drain (Kamen

1991). Traditional food processing generally does not remove the seed coats and hulls from foods. Not all traditional foods of northwestern Mexico were mentioned here. But they all contribute to the overall health and nutrition of Indigenous people in the region. They are high in fiber, low in cholesterol, and offer glucose- and insulin-controlling benefits. Together they comprise a diet that prevents many modern diseases.

Conclusion

In many ways foods reflect culture. The stories, taboos, ceremonies, and human interactions surrounding food are portholes into the myriad fascinating ways in which people relate to their diet, their natural environment, and to each other. Nutrition is secondary to the ways in which people control food production and procurement, and determine when to eat certain foods, how to prepare foodstuffs, and which foods they will or should eat. The Rarámuri gentleman who brought the bag of beans, corn, and squash to the American traveler knew that those foods are what his people have always eaten. In some way he understood that the food in the bag was directly related to the renowned stamina of his people. Yet he would not be able to describe exactly why this is so, but only that it is important for him to grow and eat the food.

At present the nutritional benefits of Indigenous foods are highlighted in clinical studies and health magazines. The nutritional aspects of the foods have risen to a more important level than the social ones. We often neglect the social dimension—the people and their cultural models—when we clinically study foods. When my walking companion assured himself that I was a corn beer drinker, he was not considering the nutritional aspects afforded by corn beer; instead, he only wanted to make sure he could invite me to a *tesguinada* so that he and I together could fulfill our ceremonial duties as Rarámuri. As cultures assimilate into the Western standard of living, several health indicators decline. It is no mystery that traditional foods and physically active lifestyles can be a key to good health. But in order for the traditional foods and lifestyles to be accepted, people must feel that they are important in their lives. Cultural aspects surrounding food and lifestyles as well as reminders of the importance of physical exercise in maintaining health and vitality can be the means of inspiring people to return to traditional foods.

In northwest Mexico plant and cultural abundance persist. Traditional diets survive as well as the people who subsist on them. The traditional foods are accessible and continue to be grown and harvested. Modernization's long tentacles have not yet completely penetrated the far reaches of the region. As a result the cultures rely on food from the land to fight off the diseases of Western culture. The Rarámuri are a model of good eating as long as their land, foods, and societies remain viable.

REFERENCES

Anderson, James W. "Dietary Fiber and Human Health." *Hort-Science* 25(1990):1488–95.

Beals, Ralph L. *The Aboriginal Culture of the Cahita Indians.* Ibero-Americana, vol. 19. University of California Press, 1943.

Beiner, Barry. "Despair on the Reservation." *Traxx Health* (December/January 1991):5–6.

Bennett, Wendell and Robert Zingg. *The Tarahumara: An Indian Tribe of Northern Mexico.* University of Chicago Press, 1935.

Brand, Janette C.B., Janelle Snow, Gary P. Nabhan, and A. Stewart Truswell. "Plasma Glucose and Insulin Responses to Traditional Pima Indian Meals." *American Journal of Clinical Nutrition* 51(1990):416–20.

Brody, Jane E. "To Preserve Their Health and Heritage, Arizona Indians Reclaim Ancient Foods." *New York Times,* May 21, 1991, B5.

Brown, David E., ed. *Biotic Communities: Southwestern United States and Northwestern Mexico.* University of Utah Press, 1994.

Bye, Robert A. "Quelites: Ethnoecology of Edible Greens—Past, Present, and Future." *Journal of Ethnobiology* 1(1981):109–23.

_____. "Incipient Domestication of Mustards in Northwest Mexico." *Kiva* 44(1979):237–55.

Cowen, Ron. "Seeds of Protection: Ancestral Menus May Hold a Message for Diabetes-Prone Descendants." *Science News* 137 (1990):350–51.

Fayhee, John. "Beating Feet and Pounding Brews with the Tarahumara." *Rocky Mountain Sports & Fitness Magazine* (September 1987):11–13.

Felger, Richard and Kevin Dahl, eds. "Northern Sierra Madre Occidental and its Apachian Outliers: A Neglected Center of Biodiversity." Unpublished report. The Drylands Institute, and Native Seeds/SEARCH, Tucson, Arizona, 1994.

Gentry, Howard S. "The Warihio Indians of Sonora-Chihuahua: An Ethnographic Survey." Bureau of American Ethnology, Bulletin 186, Anthropological Papers No. 65. Smithsonian Institution, 1963.

Harbottle, Garman and Phil C. Weigand. "Turquoise in Pre-Columbian America." *Scientific American* 266(1992):78–85.

Heiser, Charles B. "Some Botanical Considerations of the Early Domesticated Plants North of Mexico." In *Prehistoric Food Production in North America,* ed. by Richard I. Ford, pp. 57–72. University of Michigan, Museum of Anthropology, 1985.

Jackson, M. Yvonne. "Diet, Culture, and Diabetes." In *Diabetes as a Disease of Civilization: The Impact of Culture Change on Indigenous Peoples,* ed. by Jennie R. and Robert S. Young Roe, pp. 381–406. Mouton de Gruyter, 1994.

Johnson, Jean B. "The Opata: An Inland Tribe of Sonora." University of New Mexico Press, 1950.

Justice, James W. "The History of Diabetes Mellitus in the Desert People." In *Diabetes as a Disease of Civilization: The Impact of Culture Change on Indigenous Peoples,* ed. by Jennie R. and Robert S. Young Row, pp. 69–127. Mouton de Gruyter, 1994.

LeFerriére, Joseph E. "Vegetation and Flora of the Mountain Pima Village of Nabogame, Chihuahua, Mexico." *Phytologia* 77(1994): 102–12.

Minnis, Paul E. "Famine Foods of the North American Desert Borderlands in Historical Context." *Journal of Ethnobiology* 11(1991):231–56.

Nabhan, Gary P. *Gathering the Desert.* The University of Arizona Press, 1985.

_____. "Indigenous Perception and Management of Plant/Animal Relationships: The Ethnoecology of Interaction Diversity." Paper presented at the Biodiversity and Native North American Symposium, University of Oklahoma, Norman, Oklahoma, February 21, 1997.

Nelson, Ben A. "Complexity, Hierarchy, and Scale: A Controlled Comparison between Chaco Canyon, New Mexico, and La Quemada, Zacatecas." *American Antiquity* 60(1995):597–618.

_____ and Roger Anyon. "Fallow Valleys: Asynchronous Occupations in Southwestern New Mexico." *Kiva* 61(1996):275–94.

Nentvig, Juan. *Rudo Ensayo.* Trans. by Alberto Francisco Pradeau and Robert R. Rasmussen. University of Arizona Press, 1980.

Pennington, Campbell W. *The Tepehuan of Chihuahua: Their Material Culture.* University of Utah Press, 1969.

Pérez de Ribas, Andres. *My Life Among the Savage Nations of New Spain* (1644). Trans. by Tomas A. Robertson. Ward Ritchie Press, 1968.

Pfefferkorn, Ignaz. *Sonora: A Description of the Province.* Trans. by Theodore E. Treutlein. University of Arizona Press, 1989.

Ramamoorthy, T.P., Robert Bye, Antonio Lot, and John Fa. *Biological Diversity of Mexico: Origins and Distribution.* Oxford University Press, 1993.

Salmón, Enrique. "Cures of the Copper Canyon: Medicinal Plants of the Tarahumara with Potential Toxicity." *Herbalgram* (Summer 1995):44–55.

_____. "Iwigara: A Rarámuri Cognitive Model of Biodiversity and its Effects on Land Management." Paper presented at the Biodiversity and Native North American Symposium, University of Oklahoma, Norman, Oklahoma, February 21, 1997.

_____. "Tarahumara Healing Practices." *Shaman's Drum* 24(Summer 1991):34–42.

Simpson, H.C.R., S. Lousley, M. Greekie, R.W. Simpson, R.D. Carter, T.D.R. Hockaday, and J.I. Mann. "A High Carbohydrate Leguminous Fibre Diet Improves All Aspects of Diabetic Control." *The Lancet* 1(1981):1–5.

Smith, Cynthia J., Elaine M. Manahan, and Sally G. Pablo. "Food Habit and Cultural Changes Among the Pima Indians." In *Diabetes as a Disease of Civilization: The Impact of Culture Change on Indigenous Peoples,* ed. by Jannie R. and Robert S. Young Roe, pp. 407–33. Mouton de Gruyter, 1994.

Spicer, Edward H. *Pascua: A Yaqui Village in Arizona.* University of Chicago Press, 1940.

_____. "Potam: A Yaqui Village in Arizona, Part 2." *American Anthropologist* 56(1954).

Wolfe, Wendy S. "Dietary Change Among the Navajo." In *Diabetes as a Disease of Civilization: The Impact of Culture Change on Indigenous Peoples*, ed. by Jennie R. and Robert S. Young Roe, pp. 435–49. Mouton de Gruyter, 1994.

Zingg, Robert M. "Report on Archaeology of Southern Chihuahua." University of Denver, Center for Latin American Studies, 1940.

6

A Navajo's Meditations on Food and Culture

Lawrence Shorty

> *When we eat*
> *Other peoples' food*
> *We begin to think and become*
> *Like them.*

Navajo woman tossing corn in roasting pit. Photograph © Marcia Keegan.

I magine two Navajos riding around in a fancy pickup truck, laughing and telling stories: that's my grandfather and me. Neither of us lives on the Navajo reservation. Actually, both of us live in a developed area on the west side of Albuquerque, New Mexico. The first time Grandpa Shorty and I rode around together in his truck I was ten years old. I had spent the night at his house, and we woke up early to run errands in the city, and we had "fried chicken from Kentucky" for lunch.

Today, when Grandpa Shorty and I drive together we discuss how much the world has changed since he was a boy. He teaches me about the Navajo meaning of places, names, and language. I tell him what I understand, and, like a kind grandfather he corrects me, but not before laughing really hard. Instead of fried chicken, we now order it baked. We eat Vietnamese soups and vermicelli salads. Because he has diabetes, Grandpa Shorty is careful not to eat foods with too much sodium, fat, or sugar. Perhaps one day, I will also become diabetic. This is one reason why we talk: to understand how our foods and our lives have changed.

Being Navajo, my grandfather loves his truck. During one of our conversations Grandpa Shorty and I talked about automobiles and the vehicles he has owned. Although he prefers trucks, my grandfather has also owned cars. My grandfather tells me, because I haven't lived on the reservation since I was very young, that the rural roads require sturdy trucks. He tells me that Navajos use their trucks to transport people, fuel, water, livestock, and food. Take a visit to Window Rock, the Navajo Nation capital, and see all the trucks for yourself. Without a doubt, pickups are a necessity.

So, I had to ask him, doesn't anybody walk anymore? The Navajo language describes where a person lives as "the place where that individual is walking around." But most of the people I see on the Navajo reservation aren't walking, unless they're walking behind sheep. Perhaps our language should accommodate the blessing of not having to walk everywhere, I say to Grandpa. Perhaps we should describe where we live as not the place where we walk around, but rather the place from where we drive our *chidi* (car).

Here we are driving around in a pickup truck, not walking, discussing our culture, and talking about eating Asian food and being careful about what we eat. I ask him, "How about Vietnamese, for some *pho tai* [soup]? Or what about the new buffet place? I hear it has a frozen yogurt bar." "Okay," Grandpa says, "but I need to watch my sugar."

I remember being taught that food is good and wouldn't hurt me. When I was ten, breakfast with Grandpa included fried bacon, eggs cooked in bacon fat, toasted white bread smothered in butter and jam, and a bit of coffee to go with the sugar and cream. Today, breakfast with Grandpa is a boiled egg, wheat toast with margarine, and a halved grapefruit.

Another example of the Navajos' changing relationship to food involves their traditional tobacco, *nat'oh*. Nat'oh, considered a food because it is ingested, encompasses many plants, each having specific attributes. If a person wants to be luckier, she would get one type of nat'oh. If one wanted to possess greater concentration powers, he would get another type, and so on. Nat'oh provided nourishment for the mind, heart, and body. The nat'oh plants used in ceremonies pertain to certain animals and are not the commercially available tobacco products. When we use a specific type, we take into ourselves the attribute the plant contains.

Certain Native activists and politicians defend tribal-owned tobacco shops by asserting that the tobacco products they sell are sacred. This has become the reality for many Natives. But these products are not the traditional nat'oh, the sacred plants used in ceremonies. In the case of tribal-owned tobacco shops, the important concept is economic development, not sacredness. Many Native people have learned to accept commercial tobacco products as a substitute for their "real" tobacco, and have rationalized the switch from ceremonial to hedonistic use. Use of this new food is resulting in high rates of tobacco-related illness among Natives.

We have replaced what we need with what we want, and as much as we want. We have also transformed the ceremonial use of nat'oh to hedonistic consumption of commercialized tobacco products. Not surprisingly, poor diet, lack of physical exercise, and smoking large quantities of chemical-laced tobacco have contributed to chronic diseases. Navajo elders say, "When we eat other peoples' food we begin to think and become like them. Eat more and we will 'forget' how to be Navajo." Our lives have, in fact, become in large part like those of the non-Native population.

Changing Relationships to Food

Navajo stories indicate which foods are given specifically to the Diné for survival. The first food types were gathered or hunted.

My grandfather talks about the small wild potatoes, spinach, and carrots he was taught to find. I have heard from other Navajo sources stories about how small groups of people traveled to different areas to retrieve vegetables and to hunt game. Our ancestors' relationship with food was derived from their knowledge of plant and animal species zones and development patterns. Our stories tell us that the Holy People taught us dryland farming methods, and we grew corn, squash, beans, and melons. Other sources say Navajo people learned agriculture from the Pueblo people.

In the 1600s the Navajo people's lives changed dramatically. Sheep introduced into the region by the Spaniards and Mexicans became the basis of a new subsistence economy for the Navajo; material wealth came to be measured by the number and the quality of sheep and goats a family owned. Acquiring food became easier because Navajos could graze their livestock near where they lived, and where they grew or gathered vegetables and other plants. Having sheep meant that the people didn't have to chase game as much as before.

However, the new economy contributed to Navajos being imprisoned at Fort Sumner. In 1864 thousands of Navajos were forced to leave their land in Arizona and march nearly 300 miles east to an internment camp, Fort Sumner, at Bosque Redondo, New Mexico. Because soldiers burned their crops and drove away their livestock, the Navajos were effectively forced to follow the soldiers to the fort or face starvation. Many people died during the Long Walk, and subsequent lack of adequate food and shelter. After four years of confinement, they were allowed to return home to what eventually became the Navajo reservation. As a result of encroachment on their land, and because sheep had become a measure of wealth for the

Navajo people, Navajos had engaged in raiding of livestock from Anglo, Mexican, and Pueblo people. Consequently, preventing raiding was one of the rationales used by the U.S. government for the uprooting of the Navajo people. During the four years of internment, the Navajos who survived learned new habits, including how to prepare the foreign foods provided by the U.S. government. Navajos had to change or die because they were dispossessed of their land, lifestyle, and the food that had nourished them for generations. I have been told that many Navajos died trying to eat the new foods because the food made them sick. Navajos then developed fry bread, a food that today symbolizes the people's determination and innovation, and which is now understood to be part of the Navajo "traditional" diet. Like the adage, "When life gives you lemons, make lemonade," Navajos could claim, "When the federal government gives us flour, we will not starve: we will make fry bread."

Game, corn, and gathered vegetables and herbs were replaced with wheat flour, coffee, bacon, and sugar. The Navajos who survived Fort Sumner incorporated these foods into their diet. Corn tortillas were replaced by the wheat flour variety, or completely substituted with fry bread. Sugar is still considered a treat and seems to be available everywhere. Coffee is found in most homes and at ceremonies. Pork is one food that did not take hold to the same extent as the others mentioned. To the Navajo, the value of sheep far outweighs that of an animal which can only be eaten. But Grandpa Shorty loves bacon for his breakfast.

Once Navajos developed the new technology to change wheat flour into fry bread and incorporated other commodities into their diets, their lives became easier. Few Navajos walk when we can drive. Most people would never consider walking to the mesa or near the mountains to find food when it is much easier to drive to a grocery store. Our lives continually become easier. However, we must ask, at what price?

Few Navajo people today have the capability and esoteric knowledge to live off of Navajo traditional foods. The diet of the few who do is likely supplemented by "modern" foods. Some areas where subsistence foods once grew are now contaminated because of mining or other extractive industries, or else the land has been overgrazed.

Reflections on Ancient Teachings and More Recent Farming Practices

The Holy People prescribed for us the proper foods to eat and taught us how to gather them. Intertwined with those lessons are others on how Navajos should live. For example, like people, plants should be treated well, especially those that will be used in ceremonies. Treating plants with care means making prayers and offerings to acknowledge their importance and potency. Offerings show that we are conscious of our interdependence with plants and other living beings.

We are taught that when we gather herbs or food, we should only acquire what is needed from the plant. To do otherwise would be wasteful. We should also avoid appropriating all that is available from a single plant. In removing all the leaves, we may unnecessarily kill it. In an area inhabited by many plants, we are told that taking all of those plants would be selfish. Our greed would jeopardize the future of the plants because some plants must remain to flower and go to seed. We would also compromise our own future because we may eliminate what we need for our ceremonies, as well as food for the following year. Perhaps to deter us from selfishly taking all the wild plants, Navajos were taught to plant food crops. The Holy People showed us how to cultivate seeds so that we could provide our own food. This vital undertaking requires that we begin the process with prayer. Through prayer we acknowledge our intent by speaking to the earth, the seeds, the clouds, and the water, informing these elements of what we are about to do. This process both fosters and recognizes our relationship to that which we are dependent on for our survival.

For Navajos to have the potential for healthy plants and a plentiful harvest, we need to create a foundation based on prayer. As discussed earlier, our prayers build on knowledge given to us by the Holy People. This knowledge is transmitted from one generation to the next, passed on from the elders to their children and grandchildren. Our prayers indicate that we have already envisioned positive outcomes and have or are willing to gain the knowledge necessary to realize the primary goal: to supply our families with nourishing food. This signifies intent with the capacity to achieve the intent.

Like other elders, Grandpa Shorty talks about how life was different when he was a boy. For example, Grandpa Shorty's food came from what he and his family could grow with careful preparation. He said that preparing the field is one of the first and most important steps of farming, which includes considering the types of crops to be planted, the size of the area to be cultivated, and how the crops are to be watered. In addition to thinking about these issues, we would also need to address prayers to the Holy People asking for their blessing so that our fields will provide.

Navajo stories address the question of when to begin sowing seed. The Pleiades star cluster (in the Taurus constellation) indicates when we can plant. During the winter months the six stars of the Pleiades visible to the naked eye can be seen. Throughout the spring, the stars become fainter as the season progresses. Ideally, farmers offer prayers during this period as a means of spiritual and mental preparation.

The oldest method of planting uses a special wooden stick called a *gish*. Navajo farmers explain that care must be taken in preparing a planting stick. It should be a stick that will last for the duration of the season. Ideally, the gish will be sturdy but not cumbersome, and it is to be used for its intended purpose and nothing else. The planting stick is a holy tool because it is employed in planting crops such as the sacred corn. Some people say that the stick should be kept hidden near the field. A gish should not be carelessly left lying around where it could be damaged.

Traditionally, men would press the end of the planting stick into the earth to make a hole. Women followed the men, dropping seeds into the impressions. Meanwhile, the planters sang about their crop, about their joy of being in the field, and about their thankfulness for being able to farm. In some areas, field sowing was a communal event that brought different families together to pray, plant, and laugh.

People shared food at planting time. Whatever amount of food people could afford to provide was happily received. Some families were wealthy with sheep, surpluses of stored corn, and store-bought commodities. Others could only contribute a small amount. Regardless of taste or appearance, insulting food was considered improper, for the calories nourished the family who helped or would help others in their fields. Speaking negatively about a family's particular offering showed disrespect for the prayers, labor, and love that went into the preparation and planting of crops.

Many farmers planted crops by beginning in the middle of the field, spiraling out toward the boundaries. This practice suggested the strength inherent in cyclical continuity. Other farmers created straight rows, which is the most common method used today.

Planting was accompanied with songs that signify commitment to the field and to the crops. Planting songs encourage the seeds to grow. The positive feelings that emanate from the songs construct a reality for the plants, as well as for the water, sun, and soil that nurture them. The construction of reality through song reinforces the notion that all things, including the plants, animals, humans, and the Holy People are interdependent and important. For example, one planting song inspires the corn to grow strong. The words reaffirm how corn receives its water from the clouds and the morning dew. A seed cultivated with water, soil, and prayers creates life. When the corn is strong, Navajos become strong.

Consider the interdependent relationship among the Navajos' first cultivated plants—corn, beans, and squash. Squash spreads itself over the ground with its broad leaves and consequently, discourages growth of other plants. Bean vines wind themselves around corn stalks. Without corn, a bean plant would not be able to pull itself off the ground. The planting song mentioned earlier speaks to how the corn and beans interact. The corn's roots, leaves, tassel, and silk exist along with the bean plant. As the beanstalk coils around the corn plant, it provides nutrients for the nitrogen-hungry corn. Corn shares its pollen with beans and squash, which is a very sacred blessing. Perhaps the pollen blessing encourages beans to coil closely to corn.

I have heard many people talk about the differences between traditional and large-scale commercial methods. The traditional methods bring the grower into intimate contact with the soil, sun, and water. In contrast, machinery separates people from the natural world. The metal appendages that touch the soil, seeds, and plants do not actually feel or speak to the natural elements. When food is planted by hand, prepared through prayer, and cared for with the sincerest intentions and songs, the feeling invoked is vastly different from seeds planted by machine: plants cannot hear the farmer's songs of thanks over the roar of engines and the clashing noise of machinery.

My maternal grandfather, Dooley Shorty, grew up planting traditionally. My paternal grandfather, John Clay, was raised planting with more modern methods. Both have said agriculture is difficult. Success is dependent on the thoroughness of a farmer's preparation. However, careful planning will not always guarantee a good crop.

Grandpa Clay commented that "Farming is hard work and there will be times when you'll feel tired, even mad. But every time you finish with something you feel better." Grandpa and Grandma Clay would always comment how good they felt seeing their hard work transform their farm into a viable source of food crops. This positive feeling also applies to other food sources, such as livestock.

Grandfather Shorty remembers how his mother spoke about the sheep she owned. My great grandmother and other people of her generation felt a deep sense of pride and joy regarding their livestock. Grandpa Shorty recalls that his mother would tell him that sheep were also his mother, in the sense that they were providers. From sheep and goats came meat and milk. From the wool or coat, blankets could be woven. The sheepskin, too, provided warmth. Nearly every part of the sheep was used. Families who contributed meat and/or rugs from the family flock to celebrations or ceremonies reinforced the connection between people and animals. Sheep relied on people for protection, food, and water, and people relied on sheep for wealth, clothing, and food.

Attitudes Toward Food

When Navajos spend a lot of time with others, they learn their ways as a means of survival. Many Navajos live in a society vastly different from that of their elders. We live in an era when many people, including myself, do not fully understand or have access to the Holy People's teachings. As a result we are unsure about how we should treat food, and subsequently, how to treat one another. Many young Navajos do not understand the importance of food and attitudes toward food, especially during ceremonial times.

During a *kinaalda,* one of the Navajo people's most important ceremonies, corn is ground into meal, mixed with other ingredients, and baked by a girl who is making the transition to womanhood. In the course of this event a girl is prepared for adulthood and for becoming the foundation of her future family. Dried corn is worked into meal using stone presses. The cornmeal is combined with water and mixed into a batter poured into corn shucks. Next, the batter is placed into a fire-heated pit. Later, the cornmeal mixture is reborn from the earth in corn shucks as the kinaalda blessing cake, and is offered to everyone present.

The puberty ceremony brings together men and women who utilize the Holy People's teachings to create and sustain strong Navajo women. Throughout the ceremony, elders' prayers and their specific instructions and physical manipulation shape the girl. The prayers serve to bless the ceremony and retell Navajo history, which thereby reaffirm the meaning of our existence. Singing accompanies the grinding, which assists in the transformation of the corn and the girl. She is instructed by the women in her family on how to care for herself and provide for her family. The girl's aunts and grandmothers manipulate her body, furthering her metamorphosis. The women infuse their touch with strength. Blessings bring blessings.

The kinaalda ceremony reinforces our understanding that women and corn are the foundations of Navajo culture. Women are the central pillar of a family's stability. Likewise, corn upholds and blesses beans and squash for helping the corn develop into a powerful plant. In a larger sense then, both women and corn are the nucleus of Navajo existence. Navajos receive blessings from women's work. Navajos also receive blessings from corn that gives its flesh and pollen for people to eat and use in ceremonies. Both corn and women are nurtured with careful preparation and prayer.

Other foods are found at ceremonies. Navajo stews are very popular because they bring together elements of our culture. Wild spinach, potatoes and carrots, corn, and sometimes beans and squash are combined with wild or domesticated meat. Fire and water bring the stew to life. Combined with ceremonies, stew reinforces the survival and triumph stories found in ceremonial songs because it consists of foods that nurtured the formation of the Navajo people. Our ceremonies reconstruct a balanced world and the ceremonial foods help to realize it.

This is the reason people laugh and enjoy each other during these special times. They are being restored by the good intentions echoed in the prayers, discussions, and food. An important lesson I have learned from Navajo elders, and which bears repeating, is that people should never insult food. A friend of mine prides herself on her diet, fitness, regimen, strength, and ability to compete in triathlons. Although she feels good about what she eats, she admits her favorite foods are higher in fat. She restrains herself from indulging while she is in training. When we eat together at a restaurant, she spends her time looking at the menu decrying the fatty and "heavy" foods, which are therefore too "gross" for her to eat. Despite knowing that she did not truly believe that the food was disgusting, I felt insulted. The same foods that she insulted constituted my dinner.

A Navajo friend places a high value on the aesthetics of food. He is a vegetarian, something of a rarity among Natives. He is also an urban-raised person, something not so rare these days. He only eats food that looks good and is familiar. In other words, meals must be made of vegetables, breads, or pasta. He has told me about how much he hated to eat the foods his family from the reservation prepared. He obviously did not like "reservation foods" such as mutton, fry bread cooked in lard, and any kind of stew containing meat. My friend also critiqued his family's reservation lifestyle. He complained that there was nothing to do on the reservation, the hogans appeared dirty, and the people seemed mentally slow because their English pronunciation was nothing like his. He did not understand why his family continued to offer him so many meat-based foods when they knew he was a vegetarian. My friend wondered why, when he asked for "something with vegetables," his aunt gave him stew. I asked my friend what they said when they gave the dish to him. They told him, "Eat this, it's good for you. You can take the meat out."

My friend failed to realize that his family was happy to be with him and wanted to show him their joy by sharing their favorite foods. On the one hand, he felt insulted because of what he was served. On the other, he insulted the food and his family's intentions. When food is offered it should be accepted because it is presented as a means of expressing gratitude and reflects what the providers can give. If a person does not accept the food it is like saying that they do not wish to share in the host's blessings. It is to say that the host's good fortune is not worthy of observance.

Blessings come in different forms. When we recognize an event worth celebrating we are happy to have people share our food. Navajo people will even share processed foods that are not very nutritious, and the recipients are appreciative. Although many processed foods are extremely high in fat, sugar, and/or sodium, people who make such offerings may, in fact, survive primarily because of those foods. Such foods constitute their blessings, and for the little they have, they are thankful. My grandfather reminds me that they are sharing the little they possess, and that I should be thankful. Blessings build upon blessings.

Advantages of Traditional Ways

There is something special about being able to provide food that one has raised for a celebration or ceremony. We want to know where our food comes from. I wonder how many people prefer to eat food prepared with care at a loved one's home, rather than cooked at a restaurant by an anonymous worker?

In the past, physical activity was a part of necessary daily tasks, such as chopping wood, herding sheep, hauling water, farming, grinding corn, and gathering food. My Grandpa Shorty says that the way he grew up, performing that type of work to have something to eat, hardened him and made him strong. He also says that when he entered the Marines during World War II, he didn't suffer as much as other recruits because he had already endured having to work for his subsistence like his ancestors did.

According to Navajo teachings, when people work hard for their food they will have enough of what they need. When people work hard for something, usually they will show a great deal of respect for themselves and their accomplishment. And they will also respect food.

Some Native peoples are making special efforts to retain their special relationships to subsistence foods, and thereby guarantee their biological and cultural survival. Yup'ik elders, for instance, want their children to know about the tribe's traditional subsistence foods, and thus concepts of themselves in relation to their environment. Before Yup'ik children become adults, they are instructed in coordinating their positions on the earth using the stars, gun safety knowledge, and how to gather or catch subsistence foods. Despite not having access to their subsistence foods, my Yup'ik friends assert that they have a choice about what they choose to eat.

Practicalities

Very few Navajo live the subsistence lifestyle for the practical reason that it is no longer required. Grandpa Shorty says that most young Navajos couldn't live like that, and if they did, they would be complaining the entire time.

Most people work for a company or business owned by someone else, but it is not a comfortable lifestyle. Fewer people farm or are able to raise their own food. I don't have to work directly for my food. Like most people, I am compensated for work I do, which allows me to purchase beyond my needs. This doesn't mean I make a lot of money, but rather that I am able to choose to eat foods that exceed my daily requirements.

In the words of my Grandpa Shorty, "This modern day society is too fast!" This world is fast and we do have many "conveniences" that contribute to our conscious or unconscious desire for an easier life. I have heard the elders' teachings and understand their value, but I do not have the time to live as I have been directed. On most days Grandpa Shorty admonishes me for not taking enough "good time" for myself. He says that I am doing "too much running around and not eating," that is, not treating my body well, and therefore I often get tired.

Grandpa says that it bothers him that people, meaning me, are not taking the time to honor the food they eat. Having good food to eat is taken for granted by people who can eat what they want. I realized that I had not been thankful for what I have, for what really nourishes me, such as good health, good food, and great family and friends. On most days, however, I don't recognize what I have because I am too busy.

As a society, Natives included, we can now get foods "made

for running" from restaurant drive-ups. These foods, for the most part, are inexpensive and driver friendly. Food retailers are constantly developing foods to accommodate our rushed lifestyle. We have fast cars or trucks that we use to take us to work and other appointments. Meanwhile, we can listen to books on tape, type a memo on our laptop PCs, or catch our favorite "airwave philosopher" on the automobile's radio.

We know that physical inactivity contributes to obesity, and that implementing an exercise regimen can control some forms of diabetes. But like most people with rushed lives, Navajos may have difficulty finding time for an exercise regimen. If we have cars we will most likely choose to drive when we could walk because we don't want to take the time to walk.

My friends and I rush through our days and homemade dishes are cherished because of their rarity. Our busy lives do not allow the time needed to prepare the foods we love. Many of us meet the day running. Kids are whisked off to school, and parents rush to work. We rush through the day trying to meet daily deadlines so that we can rush around with our families on the weekend. Prepackaged "snack packs" are breakfast. Coffee is served in spill-proof canisters made for travel. Microwaveable foods are widely available and can be cooked without supervision, liberating people to busy themselves with other activities.

I want the time to cook my favorite meals for people I care about. However, what I desire and what I have to do sometimes conflict. For example, angry feelings can ruin a meal. Once my girlfriend made a special request for dinner. It was my turn to cook, but I had immediate deadlines that I did not remind her about. My initial reaction was to beg off and have her cook or pick up some prepared food. Instead, I chopped, diced, marinated, sautéed, and frapped for at least an hour. All the while I was becoming more and more angry because I felt my partner could have very easily cooked this meal or any other. The finished meal only slightly resembled what the glorious dish was supposed to look like. I threw down the meal, quickly filled our plates, and without saying any thanks or grace, started eating. Within a few bites we were arguing. The intensity of the fight ruined the dinner and the evening, and made working difficult. To top things off, we both got some sort of stomach flu. An aunt told me that when preparing for anything of importance, a person should avoid working when angry or holding any negative feelings about what they're trying to accomplish. When a person has ill feelings, the negativity's essence spoils the outcome and can linger like a bad aftertaste.

Resolutions

Navajo teachings say that individuals cause their own problems. For example, when a Navajo goes to see a traditional illness diagnostician, the practitioner asks, "What have you done?" This inquiry is to determine if a taboo, such as treating food poorly, has been broken. Once the cause is determined, then the necessary steps toward a cure can be administered. If we continue to allow ourselves to become ill from our actions, we will have to continue saying, "We have done it to ourselves," until we alter our lifestyles.

I ask Grandpa how he deals with his new low-fat, low-sugar, and low-sodium diet. After all, one description of a Navajo is "the one with the salt shaker in front of his (her) plate." Grandpa Shorty responds, "I pray. Every day I pray. That's how Navajos should be in this modern life."

I have been taught by my Navajo elders, the people who claim me, that praying in the morning helps establish the path for my day. Lately, I have prayed about food: not for more food, but to remember and understand what I've been taught and am learning about what we eat. Through prayer, I am able to relate what has happened in previous days and convert that information into strength to apply to the present. In thinking about my prayer, I can evaluate my goals and intentions through what has already occurred. Thus, the preparation, realization, and reflection are all essential parts of the prayer cycle.

Prayer enables Navajos to build on our ancestors' foundations. As we participate in the ancient ways, we strengthen our own foundations. Indeed, the ancient ways exist in contemporary times and enable us to utilize our own ways to accommodate social and technological change. Navajos have always met challenges directly, which is one of our most positive attributes.

Larger numbers of grocery stores are now on the Navajo reservation. In these stores, Navajos can get healthful, unprocessed foods. While they are not Navajo subsistence foods, they will be worthwhile in helping to reduce obesity and to delay the onset of diabetes. If we don't change our eating habits and our relationships to food, we will continue to be the cause of our problems.

My grandfather has shown me that it is possible to change eating habits. More importantly, he has shared Navajo teachings that will continue to shape my life and influence my relationships. This intergenerational sharing is essential to maintaining connections to the Navajo universe. It doesn't matter that we share over baked chicken from a buffet.

Through his example, I have learned to meet my problems through prayer, and in this sense, Navajos are always preparing, always getting ready for the next challenge.

7

Reflections of a Native American Farmer

Clayton Brascoupe

Phoye Tsay Brascoupe, dog Rascal, Povi Brascoupe, and Clayton Brascoupe picking corn at Four Sisters Farm, Tesuque Pueblo, New Mexico. Photograph © Clayton Brascoupe.

I remember planting a small garden right next to our house. We did not have flood irrigation so we had to use starter plants, like many people do with tomatoes. We would haul water every evening from my uncle's house because we had no plumbing at our house. We filled the buckets at the hand pump and brought them back to the garden. Then, we transferred the water into little sprinkler buckets. We would walk between the rows watering the plants. Once their root systems were built up, they could maintain themselves.

My brothers, sisters, and I started helping in the garden when we were eight or nine years old. We started with general gardening activities, such as watering the plants and hoeing the weeds. I remember not really enjoying it much. When I was thirteen, I started working on a big commercial farm. They grew different types of vegetables such as corn, celery, onions, tomatoes, cauliflower, lettuce, carrots, and potatoes.

Through my junior high and high school years, my summers were spent working mainly on a particular farm, and this is when I started to really enjoy farming. Normally, I would start on June 20. As the people on the farm began to see me as a hard worker who could do a lot of things for them, they started hiring me earlier in the year. I started working at the beginning of spring around Easter. I worked in the greenhouse, preparing the potatoes for planting. I learned how to get things started, and how and when to transplant different plants. They had this amazing machine that would transplant things. Another guy and I used to sit there day after day transplanting all kinds of plants.

At this time, I would talk to my aunts and uncles about farming. All of us lived pretty close to one another. As I got older, still in my early teens, I started listening to other people in the community talk about farming and what it meant to us as Indian people. The sharing of these stories was one way they encouraged us to farm.

I had the opportunity to work on other farms. I did some traveling and worked on a couple of farms where I picked, tied, and pruned grapes. I worked on commercial tobacco farms in southern Ontario, Canada. I had never worked with tobacco and it was a whole different experience. (I am now trying to learn more about tobacco growing, but I'm still at the experimental stage.) I also worked on a dairy farm maintaining the area where the cows lived.

I have always been interested in farming. As I talk to people who are farming now, a question I always ask is, "When did you start farming?" Most people started when they were younger, and they were also taking care of some chickens, cows, or pigs. That is usually where their interest in farming began. So, I guess it was the early experience and listening to the community people talk about farming and what it meant for them. They talked about eating food they had grown and how much better it was for you.

There was a dietary concern that food grown outside the community had been sprayed with chemicals. This seemed to be a big concern for community members. If one had a garden, they would offer encouragement by saying, "Yeah, you should keep it up because the food you buy in the store, they spray it with herbicides, fungicides, and pesticides."

When I was younger and working on some of those commercial farms, they were involved in using pesticides, herbicides, and fungicides. We were not that knowledgeable about what they were using. I'm sure I was exposed to a lot of hazardous stuff. I think DDT was just on the way out at the time. I remember buying a new pair of rubber boots at the beginning of every season. In the East, there is more atmospheric moisture, and it would get really humid. I would get out in the field early in the morning—probably around 7:00 AM—and everything was already damp, and it had not even rained. Anyway, I would buy new rubber boots and by the end of the season in September, those boots would be all rotted. I never really put the two together, but I think now that those pesticides, fungicides, and herbicides were part of the problem. Those chemicals probably ate through my boots. At the end of the season, my hands would also be all split and cracked. I would have tape on all my fingers, and I would still be out working. I never wore gloves and I still can't. It just feels funny to wear gloves when I am working, so I am sure that increased my exposure to the chemicals used to treat the plants.

When I was in my youthful traveling phase, I had the opportunity to work for some elderly farmers in Akwesasne, a Mohawk community. It was right over the border of upstate New York. The community lands go right up into Ontario and Quebec. The elders there had similar information to share about eating healthy foods and the concerns about spraying vegetable crops. They also had cultural concerns. They felt that we as Indian people came out of an agricultural background, and that in order to maintain our culture, we have to keep up the activity of farming. The activity of generating food for ourselves and our community also becomes a political act. We are asserting sovereignty, an area of self-sufficiency, by growing food for ourselves and our community. This concern was always in the conversations with older community members. If it was not said outright, it was implied.

By growing food for ourselves, we are asserting our political sovereignty. I did not understand this at the time, but as I grow older it becomes clearer. Through the activity of growing food for ourselves, we can regain our culture in different ways. Culture is a series of different types of values. What is valued in our Indian communities? In many Indian communities we value nature, and that leads to religious beliefs. What else does that activity of farming, of growing a garden, teach a person? One lesson learned through the activity of farming is how to observe nature. You learn about plants. You learn about the relationship of plants to plants and how they interact with one another. You learn how to identify different types of insects and how insects affect plant growth. You learn to identify those which are beneficial and those that are harmful. You begin to observe bird activity and learn how bird activity affects plant growth. You take notice of other plants outside of your agricultural area and how they affect the survival of your garden. You unwittingly become a student of nature.

In northern New Mexico they say that the best time to plant beans is when the cholla cacti start to bloom. What you are doing is planting and watching your schedule, but you are also watching what other plants are doing, such as the cacti. You are watching what the birds are doing. Are they building a nest? Are they taking care of their young? If they are, you know the warm season is coming and you can begin planting the early season crops. You begin to take notice of the sun because you are working outdoors. You are aware of when the sun comes up and when it goes down. You observe the effects the lunar cycle has on different plants. You start observing wind and cloud formations. Which way is the wind blowing? Which way are the clouds coming in? What shape are they? What color are they? You begin to predict if it's going to rain or not, often more accurately than the news reports.

Farming teaches you to observe and value natural forces. All these things start to become important to you. Then, the next thing you know, your family begins to observe them too. These things are important to you, and they become important to them. Your children begin to learn more about the insects, the birds, the winds, the clouds, the sun, and the lunar cycles. My children help me. If I begin to get involved in other activities, they are there reminding me of what needs to be done and what is happening.

Farming teaches community and family responsibility. Children become important because they are another set of eyes observing and hands helping. We hear about things happening in other communities, other cities, such as people disrespecting their children, men disrespecting women, and women disrespecting men. I feel these people should be eating a healthy diet and engaged in the activity of farming. They would then realize how important their children, spouses, and neighbors are. Through the whole process of farming you are dependent on others for help. The elders are also important. They offer guidance, share knowledge, and aid in harvest activities. Everyone in your family and community becomes very important to you. Why would you abuse them? Why would you want to neglect them? Why would you want to talk mean to them? As our elders have told us, eating a healthy diet nourishes the body and the spirit.

Through farming you learn that not only do you have to take care of your fields, but you have to care for your family and your neighbors. This is not only true for Indian communities; I have heard people talk about this in the Midwest. Farming communities are disintegrating because there are fewer and fewer people working the land. The emphasis of relying on mechanical instruments to bring a crop forth is eroding the family. The mechanical tools become more important to you than your family, so you spend more and more time tending to your machines than to your family. This is an indicator of where we are going. Things definitely need to change.

In the Iroquois communities, most of the celebrations or religious activities are either directly or indirectly tied to agriculture. So, if agriculture goes out of the community, maintaining religious ties to the natural world begins to decline. The Iroquois are more reliant upon rain, and do not use much flood irrigation. They have a strong appreciation and reverence for rain, thunder, and lightning. This is incorporated into their traditional knowledge, practices, and beliefs. When it begins to rain and if you are not involved in raising crops or plants, you complain and start cursing the rain. It interferes with your plans. We farmers, on the other hand, replace the activity we were engaged in with another without complaint. We give our thanks to the Creator for the rain and all it brings.

A relationship with the land, plants, animals, rain, thunder, and lightning makes one's religion more meaningful than simply going through the motions. Christians going to church on Sundays talk about being kind to one another but as soon as they leave the church they are observed to behave in a different manner. The Iroquois religious or spiritual beliefs are very similar to those of the Pueblos in New Mexico; both are agriculturally based. If farming is not an important part of what you are doing, the prayers and so forth also become less and less meaningful. That's the way I see it. Of course, other people can have different views and interpretations. When I'm involved in growing food and raising fruit, I have a more direct connection to what is happening in the natural world and this connection makes religious beliefs more meaningful.

The values that farming can transmit affect our education about how to live with each other. Farming teaches sharing, and sharing has always been very important in Indian communities. When I was younger more people were into farming. I can remember many of the older people sharing their food surpluses with people who did not have quite as much. You can see that when there are fewer and fewer people farming, there is less and less surplus and less and less sharing.

The idea of sharing is related to who is important in your community. I think the reason for sharing by people who farmed is because they felt their neighbors were very important to them. I feel that way now: my farming neighbors are very important to me. They say these things that you bring forth in planting are gifts of the Creator. The corn, pumpkin, chile, squash, or whatever, were given to you as gifts. You in turn can give your gifts to someone else. The ability to farm gives you the opportunity to share.

Farming teaches appropriate family living, and how you should interact in your community. These are very important values in Indian communities. Farming emphasizes positive values over negative ones, while also teaching the consequences of negative values. It shows you the positive things in life and nature, and the field or garden is a good place to learn. I like to farm because every day you learn something wonderful.

Farming makes the words of our parents, aunts, uncles, and elders in our community real. You actually see what they were talking about in their prayers. You actually see it with your own eyes and feel it in your heart. Farming would be a wonderful way to transform the conditions that people are experiencing now, such as child abuse, abuse of family members, and all the other horrible things. I think it would be a good way of altering the way people observe life and behave toward one another. Not only do I get all the benefits of learning wonderful things and bringing forth foods, I get to share them with others. I get to share with my children, my wife, and people that have an interest in growing things.

Once you start growing things, it takes you off into a whole other way of seeing the world. You have plenty of time to meditate. When you are working in the field, you have time to think about anything and everything. One of the things I have started wondering about is why I want to farm to begin with. There are less strenuous things than farming and gardening that I could do. This thought keeps popping up in my mind. I've narrowed it down a little to the influence of my grandmother. My parents, my brothers and sisters, and me lived with my Grandmother in her house. I remember my grandmother always being very happy and not wanting or desiring material things. I remember her working in her garden, living a very simple life, and eating a very simple diet. I too have discovered that contentment and happiness come from knowledge of the natural world. At this time in my life, I am content and happy, and I am constantly learning new things.

Organic Farming Techniques

Recently, I was out in the field checking pumpkin and squash plants for squash bugs. The bugs actually kill the plants, so I have to check under each plant to look for them. When I find squash bugs on the plants, I kill them. This is a way of releasing anger for me as well as pest control. There are various methods you can use to control pests in the field, and I am not sure which are new and which are old. Many of the things being discovered now were actually practices used many years ago. Some of these "discoveries" involve going into the field and doing hand work, and some are related to planting.

By timing the planting right, you may be able to miss an insect cycle. That is what they were saying about beans in terms of a good time to plant being when the cholla cacti are in bloom. One of the reasons that this is a good time involves getting into the rainy season, which means you might not have to irrigate the bean plants. Another reason involves the fact that if you plant earlier you are more likely to get more bean beetles. By planting when the cholla cacti are in bloom you miss the bean beetle's life cycle. Most beans have a short growing season, so you can still get a crop but with less insect damage.

Another method of reducing insect damage through organic methods is rotating crops from one area to another. If corn had been planted in a certain field one season, don't plant corn in that field the next year, because an insect cycle has been introduced to that area. When the insects come out in such a field the following year, some starve and some are eaten by birds. This strategy of pest control has been used for centuries and is based on observing the habits of birds and insects. The other advantage of crop rotation is maintaining soil fertility.

Regardless of the method you choose to reduce insect damage, you never want to wipe out all the bugs because there are many beneficial insects. These "beneficials" also need something to eat. If you are spraying, you are killing all the bugs and poisoning the food chain. The birds eat and feed their young poisoned bugs and plant material. The animals that feed on these birds are then affected. It goes on and on.

Intercropping is another way of maintaining balance in terms of insect populations and soil nutrients. We started experimenting with intercropping over the past few years. Rather than planting a single crop per field (monocropping or monoculture), you introduce a variety of plants to the same field. These plants are planted in close proximity to one another. What happens is that you create a balanced environment, and thus balance in insect populations, including the beneficials and the pests. The insects will then maintain that balance among themselves along with the birds.

Intercropping was something that my wife, children, and I had always discussed, but I had never really observed it in practice. One year we were talking about it, discussing what we were going to plant and how we were going to plant. Usually the farming discussions happen when we are eating our meals. I said I would pursue the intercropping subject a little further. Thus far I have experimented with a variety of crops. I am working on crop diversity and timing, trying to find the combination(s) that will work. Intercropping is a way of maintaining balance and diversity in your field. When you have balance in your field with your crops, the insects are working for you, not against you. If your soil is good, your plants will come up strong. Plants will not grow strong if the soil is imbalanced. Insects are predators: they smell this imbalance, and will then prey on the weak plants. If you have balance in the soil and balance in how you plant it, the plants will be strong. When you have all that balance, your diet then becomes balanced. When the right combination of nutrients exists in the soil, the vegetables you grow are also giving you the nourishment you need. You are eating the beans, corn, and squash, so whatever happens in the field that is good and balanced also affects your body.

Some people I talked to said that long ago their ancestors used to eat these bugs that make a buzzing sound. These bugs come out in mid-July to late August and are found in juniper trees. Anyway, the people used to harvest them, and then roast and eat them. That is another way of balancing an insect population. Another thing people have told me is that you can eat the worms found in corn. They call it a corn worm, and I think it is some kind of moth. Certain corn varieties limit the damage that the worms will do because they are tight husked and the worms have a hard time getting under the husk. I have heard this from three different sources. They said when they were harvesting corn, they would save the worms they found and cook them. Usually, they gave them to the children. The worms were helpful for any sort of stomach ailment. I have not tried this, but every year I get more and more tempted to do so. The worms have been eating nothing but corn so they must be a good source of protein.

A fungus can also infect a certain variety of corn. I have heard that even the fungus is edible. I have to inquire into that a little bit more. What I have also heard, and what I understand, is to avoid eating lunch in your field or garden as a means to reduce insect and bird damage. When you are working in your field there are usually birds around in the trees and there are also grasshoppers and other bugs around. The birds and the grasshoppers have eyes and ears, and they are watching you. They are watching what you are doing and they are listening to what you are doing. If you eat in your field they see this. They say, "We'll go over there and eat too." You are inviting them into your field. This goes back to what our elders have told us about sharing. When you are in your home and about to eat and there are people walking by or playing outside, you invite them to come inside and eat. That is basically what you are doing when you are eating in your field. You are inviting your neighbors, the grasshoppers and the birds, to come in and eat.

The Healing Power of Herbs

I have five brothers and sisters. The three brothers were real close together, and I was the youngest of the three. Our grandmother would take us out in the springtime to gather various medicinal plants. There were certain teas we would drink in the springtime to keep our bodies healthy, and some of the teas were really bitter. She would say, "If it wasn't bitter it probably wouldn't be good for you." Our grandmother would take us out to show us the plant and tell us where it grew. You have to look for certain things, such as where that particular plant grew, whether it was a wet or dry area, the types of other plants growing around it, and the types of trees in the vicinity. She would show us how to pick the plant. We were careful not to pick too much so that these plants would continue to grow and help us. We would take what we gathered home and she would prepare it.

If one of us got sick, she would take us out and show us the plant or plants that were good for that illness. As time went on, if we learned the uses for a particular plant, she would not take us anymore, but simply send us to gather it. Because all our lessons were in our native language, I do not know what most of the plants are called in English. My oldest brother has a wider knowledge of the plants and their names and where they are located than I do. He was more interested in the herbs at the time than my other brother and me.

The medicines she taught us came from herbs, vines, and the bark of different trees or bushes. She taught us that sometimes a certain plant that was good for a particular thing would have a twin, or a plant that looked just like it. However, this plant might be useless to humans or even harmful. The lookalike plant usually grew in an area where the other was not found. This is why you have to know the environment in which the plants you want can be found. When gathering mushrooms you must be extra careful because some are poisonous. The lesson here is that you must observe nature closely. I remember a particular bush; it was tall and grew really close together. When you bent its branches, they would snap, and it smelled real nice where you broke the branch. We'd collect a certain amount, bring it to the house, and my grandmother would cook it up. Anyway, there was another bush that looked just like it. When you bent the branches, they did not snap. The branches would just bend so you knew you had the wrong bush.

For each plant my grandmother would take us on a trip and tell us what the plant's name was, the type of area in which it could be found, and what it was used for. It was one trip for each plant. She showed us how to pick the plants. We would bring them home and she would teach us how to cook them. It was not like going to school, but rather a part of our lives.

Whenever illness came up we would go and pick plants like mushrooms, sassafras tea, wild onions, and a variety of berries. We learned the uses of different types of berries and where to find them. When we were hunting we would keep an eye out for different herbs. We would not collect them, but we knew where to find them in case we needed them.

The practices we learned from our grandmother taught us how to avoid being greedy. We were taught how to share not only the harvests but also knowledge of abundance. Our grandmother showed us how to harvest a variety of barks. The bark from willows is good for different things. The outside bark of basswood trees could be used for containers and rattles, and its inner bark is used to make rope and thread. The thread was used to sew corn husks together to make mats. She taught us how to take the bark off the tree without killing it. The procedure would leave a scar, but it would not kill the tree if you were careful.

I recall a time when I was harvesting basswood bark, cutting the bark from the tree. I had started from the bottom and was pulling upward to get the outside bark off. This has to be done at a certain time of the year; otherwise, you are wasting your time. Anyway, I was pulling the inside bark out and I was taking more of the outer bark off and I ended up stabbing myself with my knife. I punctured the vein that goes under the wrist, the one that makes you bleed a lot. Thankfully, the basswood tree's leaves are good for cuts. I held my wrist as I collected leaves from the tree I was working on. I chewed the leaves to make them into a paste. I rolled the paste into a ball and put it on my cut. I took another leaf and placed it over the top like a bandage. Then I took some of the inside bark I had collected and tied down the bandage. I finished harvesting the rest of the bark, rolled it up, took it home, and gave it to my grandmother. Grandmother asked me what happened to my wrist, and I told her I had cut it. It had been thirty to forty-five minutes between the time I cut myself and the time I got home. I took off the leaf and the glob of leaves that I had chewed. I could not believe it; the wound had closed up.

To gather plants properly, and to avoid hurting yourself or someone else, you have to know what you are doing. There are many plants that have many uses like the basswood tree. Take raspberries, for example: you can eat them, you can make teas from them, and they say the leaves of the raspberry are medicine. There are also plants with thorns; some have properties that will give you rashes, and some are poisonous. You have to know what is good and bad for your purposes out there.

How Can Farming Be Revived in Indian Communities?

What needs to be done to revive farming? I believe that general things need to happen on two levels. One is educating people to farming methods and a healthy diet. For example, the vegetables and fruits available in most grocery stores have been sprayed with all sorts of things. The soil on the farms that furnish these fruits and vegetables have been stripped of essential nutrients from overuse. This means that these crops are being grown more or less artificially. The pollution affects not only what you are eating but the environment as well. The process of getting food to conventional grocery stores is very destructive. People have to learn to understand this.

Lots of people are concerned about the environment. People have to be educated about how various activities affect the environment. Conventional agriculture based on petrochemical products is probably the most destructive activity human beings are forcing on the environment. Once that is understood, people can start to look at what they can do, such as growing their own food organically or supporting organic agriculture by buying organic produce. If you have a land base and you have water, you can start teaching organic farming methods.

It was mentioned earlier that people farming today started when they were very young. So what do you do? You start teaching kids sustainable agriculture when they are small. This should probably begin in the third grade when the children are eight or nine years old. How do you do that? You have to start working with schools, school boards, and communities. We need to introduce sustainable agriculture into the school curriculum. Not only will the kids learn mathematics, they will learn biology, astronomy, and chemistry. They will learn a lifesaving skill that touches on all academic subjects. That's what I'd like to see happen.

We must also make farming an economic benefit to the community. People who farm are often asked, "How do you support yourself?" Well, when people begin to support organic agriculture it becomes more viable. You can get more dollars per acre from organically grown produce compared to produce grown by petrochemical means. In petrochemical agriculture a lot of your capital leaves the farm, the family, and the community, and goes to large multinational petrochemical companies.

There are hundreds of varieties of corn available and only four types are grown on a large scale in the United States. When you become dependent on a single method like monocropping, eventually crops will fail, even with all the herbicides, pesticides, and fungicides. You will get some sort of corn blight or insect that cannot be controlled through petrochemicals. This would devastate the market, leading to skyrocketing prices. We need diversity on our farms and in our plant community in order to survive. Through organic methods we can maintain that balance, that diversity, over the long term. If we remain dependent on petrochemical means to bring crops forth we are looking at a dam waiting to burst. People have to learn these things, and hopefully they will change what they are doing. You can't simply tell people that they ought to farm or grow their own food. You can talk to people until you're blue in the face and you will not get anywhere. If they are aware of what is happening and are aware of the implications, then, I feel, people will change.

I see this happening in Tesuque Pueblo, New Mexico. There is an awful lot of farming going on and it is being done by younger people. When you see that, you see a future in farming. Once one person starts to farm, the effects of losing farmers begin to be reversed. What you have to look at is why did agriculture begin to decline in Indian communities.

We must understand why Indian people abandoned farming in order to understand how to reverse this trend. It was economics: people felt they could make more money and better provide for their families if they went to work for wages. In addition, the petrochemical farms were producing cheaper produce. (The same farms cannot maintain the same practices now, because it is going in the reverse—they are having to spend more to produce less.) These are the reasons why some of the people left the farm. They could not raise enough and be able to sell, trade, or barter it in a cash economy. Many left farming, not because they wanted to, but because it was an economic necessity. I have talked to many Native people and they have said that another reason farming declined in Indian communities was because many of the men were drafted. They went to the military, and no one was on the farm to make it work. When they came back they got jobs outside the community.

Today many people do not farm because there is a lot of emphasis on attaining success. What does it mean to succeed in life? Everyone wants to be successful, to be respected in their community. What does it take to become successful and respected? Today it means having money and material possessions. Farming is looked upon as the last resort. You are not highly regarded if you are a farmer. People feel you did not have the ability to succeed in the educational system if you are a farmer. These opinions about farming and success are promoted through the school system. We are taught to be greedy, selfish, and jealous of our neighbors and others. Such teachings are the opposite of traditional community values. These values lead us to start purchasing more. That's what people want you to do because that puts money in their pockets so they can then buy the big house or the more expensive automobile. This type of thinking is the opposite of sharing with and valuing human beings.

We can see where that value system has led us. We are reaping a complete disregard for human life because we value material and mechanical things more. We want shoes that we cannot afford. We want automobiles we cannot afford and we will do anything to get them. People even kill their children; you see that in the news. Now that we have seen where selfish materialism has taken us, do we want to continue? Do we see this value system as having a future? Some people will continue to participate in this value system, and some will say, "No, that is not right: we value human life, we value nature, we value the plants, the animals, the wind, and the stars."

Thus, we return to activities such as agriculture that reflect life-sustaining values. It is just really listening to what our elders, our culture, our stories have been trying to reinforce, even in the face of all those other things. It is tough to share what you have when you are trying to save for a really nice pair of shoes or something like that. People are looking for immediate satisfaction. It's hard for me to get into that part of the debate because I hardly buy anything myself. Most of my clothes are given to me by my wife or my children or other people. When you purchase something, you receive immediate satisfaction but it does not last. You get tired of what you bought in no time. It's like children with toys—they always want the latest thing out there. People are spending millions of dollars saying, "This is what you need, this is what you want, this is what's going to make you happy." Okay, so we go out and buy it, whatever it may be, and we are bored with it in an hour or a day or a week. So, what can satisfy us? Something else that we can spend a million dollars on? There is no real happiness buying things, so where do we get happiness? Happiness is found in the interaction of feeling valued by our families, of spending time with our mothers, our fathers, our aunts and uncles, our grandparents, and the people in our communities.

We feel valued then, highly valued. How much self-esteem do you get from purchasing the latest shirt? How much do you get from sitting down and having a meal that you not only helped plant, but helped water, cultivate and hoe, and also helped choose the seeds? A lot! There are all sorts of examples of that; I could go on and on about how this one activity could affect children in a positive way. Farming is hard work and makes you sweat, and I did not like to do it when I was younger. What we have to do is value hard work, working with our hands. No one values hard work anymore. People would rather make lots of money without doing any work. That is the ultimate goal—to possess a lot with very little effort.

Again it goes back to immediate gratification. I talked to a farmer and gardener about this once; he lived back in the hills in Oklahoma and he's now passed away. He was a well-respected person in his community, and was also what you would call a medicine man. By any standard he was very poor materially—he had holes in his pants and he did not have the latest footwear. But, he was respected in his community and internationally as well. People from all around the world used to visit him. He talked about these values and lived by them. He used to bring up this thing about immediate gratification. He said nowadays we have instant coffee, instant potatoes, instant everything. And he even said nowadays we have instant medicine men. He was talking about people immediately becoming something that takes a lifetime to achieve. He was pointing out that it had everything to do with us wanting everything right away, and not wanting to work for something. Much of the knowledge he acquired in his lifetime that people from everywhere wanted to know about was obtained while he worked in the field with a hoe in his hand. So there is a lot to be said for the activity of farming.

I have seen the knowledge this man in Oklahoma had in other people, and hopefully some of the truths will be revealed to me in my lifetime. Such knowledge comes from hard work, from not seeking immediate gratification. If nothing else, you learn patience from farming. In farming you do not receive

Phoye Tsay Brascoupe harvesting corn at Four Sisters Farm, Tesuque Pueblo, New Mexico. Photograph © Clayton Brascoupe.

immediate satisfaction: things take their time to grow and nourish with all the elements involved. Everything you achieve in your lifetime should be achieved in this way, that is, through a natural process with all the elements involved.

Even school is sort of an artificial environment—how do you maintain some type of naturalness in your education? I am not sure how to achieve or maintain connections to the natural environment in education at this point. Things that I learned in school were wonderful. However, I guess my education was not in the classroom, but at home in a more natural environment. That is what I would like to see changed so that a balance is achieved. That is where things are going to have to go.

Daybreak Farm and Food Project Seeks Revitalization of White Corn Usage

Yvonne Dion-Buffalo and John Mohawk

*John Mohawk working in the field in Iroquois country. Photograph ©
John Mohawk.*

Sixteenth-century Spanish accounts of life in Mexico after the conquest include descriptions of *tamales* (derived from the Nahuatl *tamalli*, meaning "bread wrapped in corn leaves") made with *masa*, a maize dough. After the corn kernels were hulled and softened in an alkaline lime solution, and the fillings prepared—fruits, spices, meats, beans, yellow chiles, and various combinations—the tamales were wrapped in cornhusks or other edible wrappings and then steamed until tender. These and other powerful images offer evidence that the Mexica— known to most of us as the Aztec—and other Indigenous peoples enjoyed a wonderful food culture based on corn.

Contemporary visitors to Mexico will have a difficult time finding these culinary delights and few North American chefs have ever tasted or recreated these corn treats. The Spanish conquest brought with it enormous cultural changes that extended to food. With rare exception, the tamales found today are not the same as the foods eaten by the Mexica. The Spanish brought with them the pig and a rich culinary tradition of cooking with lard. Consequently, today's tamale is a derivative of the Spanish and Indigenous traditions, and one will look long and hard for a recipe which does not include lard or, at best, a lard substitute.

Conquest and colonization initiated a legacy of food exchanges and adaptations that continues to the present. The Americas provided many of the foods which are now grown worldwide, including tomatoes, potatoes, many types of beans and squash, peppers, and peanuts. Most of us would barely recognize a pre-conquest menu, and few of us have taken time to think about how the changes in people's diets and lifestyles came about and what the impact of those changes might be.

Impact of Changing Diet and Lifestyle

At the beginning of the nineteenth century about ninety percent of the people in the United States lived in rural areas and were employed in food production. By the mid-twentieth century those percentages were reversed. What had happened in the meantime has been called the Great Transformation— from rural to urban life—and is the legacy of the industrial revolution. The move away from rural life has also affected the continent's Indigenous peoples, albeit at varying rates over time. Relatively few Indigenous people today cultivate or gather plants and/or hunt or raise animals for their subsistence. Consequently, Native American diets and lifestyles have changed, and sometimes changed radically over the course of a single generation.

The outcomes of a diet comprised of "modern" foods combined with less physical exercise are some of the world's highest rates of diabetes, heart disease, and cancer among Native American peoples. These disease patterns in certain populations have become noticeable only during the past fifty years.

Many epidemiologists believe that Indian health problems arise from the sudden shift from wild and near-wild foods to super-domesticated crops. Highly refined foods such as white flour and white sugar tend to enter and exit the blood stream quite rapidly. This means the body must rapidly produce large quantities of chemicals such as insulin. When the refined food is absorbed, the blood sugar rush is over.

Wild foods tend to take much longer to digest. Almost any plant or animal in nature must be "tougher" than domesticated crops and livestock in order to survive the rigors of climate, attack by disease and animals, and the necessity to be self-sufficient in the area of reproduction. Wild turkeys, for example, are arguably faster, smarter, and more survival proficient than their domestic relatives. The same can be said for the wild versions of domestic crops, such as corn, beans, and squashes, among many others. When we eat wild foods, as our ancestors did for untold generations, we are eating foods that are not easily and quickly digestible.

Wild and near-wild foods send sugar into the bloodstream more slowly and over a longer period of time. Such foods tend to render a person less hungry for a longer period of time, and this natural appetite suppressant may account for the lower incidence of obesity among people who live on a diet of such foods. It also may have significant health impacts. For instance, when Papago Indians—a people who suffer high rates of circulatory ailments and diabetes—return to their traditional diet of wild foods gathered in the desert and traditional food crops (e.g., corn, beans, and squash), they lose weight and their blood sugar levels significantly improve.

On the Revitalization of
Iroquois White Corn

Maize was a popular food in America during the seventeenth and eighteenth centuries because European crop varieties fared poorly in the difficult climates of the Northeast woodlands.

Iroquois white corn, a variety of flint corn, is still cultivated by Native farmers in New York state, Ontario, Quebec, and Wisconsin. This corn variety is incorporated in a wide variety of dishes, many of which are known to Natives who raise and use corn throughout the hemisphere, but generally unknown outside Indian country. There are exceptions—maize remains a staple in some parts of Appalachia and is enjoyed in certain parts of the South in the form of a dish known as "grits."

Contemporary books on Mexican cooking—even excellent cookbooks—recommend use of field corn in recipes for tamales, *tortillas,* and other dishes. Field corn is a product of the industrial revolution in agriculture: high-yield corn hybrids were developed to be easily harvested by machine, and thereby serve as inexpensive animal fodder. In contrast, Iroquois white corn was carefully selected by Native Americans over the course of many centuries as a human food. It is labor intensive, not well adapted to mechanical harvesting, and provides relatively modest yields. Therefore, it is more expensive to produce than field corn, and offers significantly higher food value.

Native American communities are an excellent source of plant varieties that have disappeared from the landscape elsewhere in the Americas. Meanwhile, however, those varieties are in danger of disappearing altogether because farming in Indian country has declined as a result of cultural and economic pressures. Native American farmers report they have difficulty marketing their crops and getting high enough prices to make small-scale farming profitable. Most report they would continue in or resume small-scale and organic farming if they could earn a decent income.

Iroquois white corn is an example of a beloved, highly nutritious plant variety that Native farmers would like to cultivate or continue cultivating, but experience difficulty marketing. Moreover, white corn processed products have very short shelf lives. To be a viable food product today, these items must have a long shelf life while maintaining high-quality taste and texture.

In the recent past, numerous programs by Natives and non-Natives have been launched to produce and market white corn, among other foods grown traditionally by Native farmers. These efforts have provided important information that has given direction to the Daybreak Farming and Food Project, organized at the State University of New York at Buffalo by certain members of the American Studies Department's Native Studies component. The plan was to find ways to market the produce of small-scale Native American growers through contacts, education, and demonstrations of their foods.

One example of information derived from previous and concurrent white corn projects is that although Iroquois people consider a soup made of corn, beans, and pork a national dish, it is fairly certain that non-Natives do not and probably will not eat large amounts of the same. Many people would rather not include pork or lard in their diets, and some would prefer to avoid animal products altogether. People involved in the Daybreak Project have made the assumption that if Iroquois white corn is to become accepted among the general public it will be as an ingredient in popular dishes, some of which will probably be invented in restaurant settings. This means that a suitable and stable white corn product must be made available to restaurants and, by extension, to individuals for cooking at home.

In March 1997, a cooking demonstration of sorts was held at the Mohawk Nation Bed and Breakfast outside Canajorharie,

New York. The food fair was made possible by collaboration of several entities, including the Collective Heritage Institute of Santa Fe, New Mexico, and Leslie McEachern of Angelica Kitchen in New York City. The Center for Mutual Learning at Smith College provided a small grant to help with transportation and other costs, and the Mohawk Nation Bed and Breakfast provided the facilities and sleeping quarters for some of the guests. About two dozen people, including Indigenous cooks, a vegan chef, and enthusiastic supporters of the idea, came together for a weekend of shared styles and recipes. The result was a weekend food fair which featured vegan-style cooking and a sampling of various appetizers, breads, and main dishes. Casseroles of many varieties, pancakes, muffins, and stews—most incorporating Iroquois white corn—were served. The event was informal and congenial but, most of all, a real transaction. Native American cooks learned about vegan cooking, and vegan cooks saw a few Native American traditional food techniques.

One of the most interesting foods presented at the fair was tamales—the Iroquois refer to them as cornbread. Tasty, nutritious, and satisfying, this food is probably a close approximation of the tamales known to the Mexica. Cornbread or tamales are also of interest because they contain no animal products of any kind and have served as a ceremonial and festive food for Indigenous peoples of the Northeast for at least a thousand years. An Iroquois cornbread is usually larger than the typical Mexican tamale. The loaves are four to seven inches in diameter and more than an inch thick. The Iroquois boil or bake their cornbread (as do some of the Native peoples of Mexico).

In late spring 1997, the Daybreak Project received a grant from the First Nations Development Institute that made possible several activities, including gathering recipes for a cook-book, creation of a web site on the Internet, and extensive experimentation and collaboration on the uses of white corn products. Two significant events resulting from the grant were participation in the annual Bioneers Conference in San Francisco in October 1997 and in another conference at the Cattaraugus Indian Reservation in western New York in January 1998.

The Daybreak Project has developed several products including Seneca Roast Corn Meal, Iroquois White Corn Flour, Iroquois Hominy Flour, and Iroquois Posole. At present, these products are familiar to few people in the food marketing and restaurant businesses. The Daybreak Project is unique because it seeks to become self-sufficient through a combination of the following activities: make versions of Iroquois white corn available to restaurant chefs, collect and publish recipes, and encourage small-scale organic farming among Native farmers.

Short-Term and Long-Term Objectives

The Daybreak Farming and Food Project was established to support, encourage, and promote traditional Native farming within the Iroquois Six Nations (Seneca, Cayuga, Onondaga, Oneida, Mohawk, and Tuscarora), and the marketing of Native farmers' products. The Project's short-term objectives are summarized below.

▲ Conduct educational seminars on how white corn is planted, harvested, and processed, and how to prepare authentic and creative dishes based on white corn, such as parched cornmeal sweetened with maple syrup and cornbread (tamale) variations.

▲ Encourage new Iroquoian growers to meet an anticipated demand for white corn and white corn products.

▲ Explore the Northeastern off-reservation markets for
Iroquois white corn and respective products.

Long-term objectives of Project participants follow.

▲ Sponsor and support food fairs that would introduce
Native American and non-Native cooks to Native cooking, while simultaneously introducing non-Native cooks
to Indigenous growers.

▲ Help establish an organic certification program that
would enable Native-grown products to be introduced
into national markets.

▲ Sponsor and support initiatives implementing trans-
national Indigenous communities' marketing networks
and programs.

▲ Help establish national marketing alliances to benefit
small-scale farmers.

Conclusion

Native American food crops are significantly closer to wild
foods than are most domesticated crops. The impact on
human health of Native-grown crops is likely not the same as
wild foods, but they are a step in the right direction. Learning
to cook such foods and to make them a regular part of people's
diets is increasingly seen as a way to better health, stronger
agriculture, and ultimately stronger communities among
certain Indigenous peoples. The end result of the Daybreak
Project and similar programs could be the reintroduction of
high-quality maize products to a wide variety of consumers

Corn is sacred to many Indigenous peoples of Turtle Island (the Americas).
Photograph © Marcia Keegan.

including restaurants, mail-order customers, and reservation and urban Natives.

Many food plant varieties grown by Native Americans are virtually unknown to people outside their communities. These and similar crops from around the world constitute the food heritage of humanity and should be preserved not only for posterity but for their biological diversity and culinary possibilities. White corn is one of the many gifts of aboriginal American agriculture which has not only a glorious past but also a wonderful future.

9

Rituals and Practices of Traditional Folk Medicine in the U.S. Southwest and Mexico

Eliseo Torres

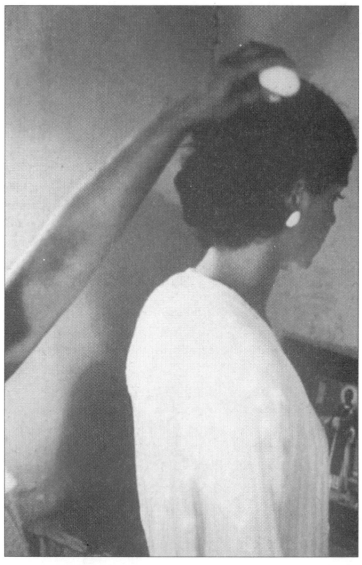

Using an egg to absorb negative vibrations during a mal de ojo *("evil eye") cleansing ritual. Photograph © Eliseo Torres.*

The term *curanderismo* may be translated as "folk healing." A curandero or curandera, then, is a healer, with the letter at the end of the word signifying male or female, respectively. All three words derive from the Spanish verb, *curar*, which means to heal. The roots of curanderismo are many. The Moors, for instance, introduced Arabic elements, which came to the New World via Spain. The theory of "the humors," with its emphasis on balance between light and darkness, and heat and cold, was introduced in this way. Some beliefs associated with curanderismo, particularly the insistence that all power to heal comes from God, are Judeo-Christian in origin. There are also powerful Indigenous—particularly Aztec (Mexica)—influences too, most often in the herbal remedies curanderos use.

Curanderismo has always embraced three levels, although certain curanderos may choose to emphasize one of the three or even exclude altogether the other two. These levels are the *material* (the most common, with its emphasis on objects such as candles, oils, herbs), *spiritual* (here the curandero is often a medium), and *mental* (e.g., psychic healers). Rituals—formulaic or patterned ways of treating the various illnesses of patients—are present on all three levels.

The use of a raw chicken's egg is quite common in curanderismo, perhaps because, as Robert T. Trotter and Juan Antonio Chavira note in *Curanderismo* (1981), "The material properties of the egg include its ordinary use as food; its mystical properties, however, include its ability to absorb negative influences (sickness) from a patient." Still another reason is that many rituals demand a sacrificial object, and, again according to Trotter and Chavira, "the egg qualifies as an animal cell." In addition to the egg, lemons figure in rituals of curanderismo, as does *agua preparada* (specially prepared water). Water, especially water that has been blessed (holy water), is considered a physical link with the spirit world. In fact, it is not uncommon for a curandera to dip other objects she is using into holy water to enhance their curative powers.

In addition, fire in the form of candles and incense plays a part in many of the ceremonies, as do many herbs (see Torres 1983) and aromatic oils. But, as with lemons and the egg, curanderismo also relies on items which are very ordinary indeed. Purple onions and garlic, for instance, are often used. These items are said to protect people, while the aforementioned egg and lemon are believed to absorb negative forces.

State of consciousness distinguishes curanderos working on the material level: they are awake rather than in a trance and are themselves—that is, they have not assumed the being of another. Material level curanderos also have specialties. A *yerbero/a* will be an herbalist, able to prescribe botanical remedies. A *partera* is a midwife. A *sobador/a* will be a masseuse or masseur. That the material, spiritual, and mental levels overlap can easily be seen when we use the sobador as an example.

The sobador might well work only on the material level, using his hands and perhaps an aromatic oil or a poultice or even a tea. But the sobador might also heal an illness that exists deep beneath the surface of the skin, perhaps in the nervous system or in the mind. That sobador might be said to operate on the psychic level as well. There are sobadores, for instance, who have been said to cure paralysis.

A *señora,* however, because she reads cards in order to fore-tell the future or reveal the influence of the past, can be said to emphasize the mental or psychic level. An *espiritista* (or *espiritualista),* often described as a medium, would work entirely on the spiritual level.

While it is true that most curanderos work on the material level, the spiritual mode is growing in popularity. This is particularly due to the *Fidencistas,* followers of Niño Fidencio, a Mexican healer. These followers are said to assume Niño's spirit now that he is dead—that is, they *become* him in order to heal.

Is belief in curanderismo a religious belief, or is it a belief in the supernatural? Well, it is often both. The aforementioned belief that all healing power comes from God makes it religious, as does the very prevalent idea that a curandero can only bring about God's will. The belief that certain rituals or practices can effect a certain outcome is, however, a belief in the super-natural—that is, a belief that outside forces can be changed or controlled. Consequently, curanderismo partakes of both the religious and the supernatural. In fact, a curandero can be a *brujo* (witch) capable of casting evil spells. Curanderismo, therefore, is careful to distinguish between white magic and black magic, with most curanderos espousing the former.

How does one become a curandero? Often, it is a matter of recognizing that one has the God-given gift—the *don,* as it is called. Sometimes, too, it is the result of a long apprenticeship. In defining who is and who isn't a curandero, the amount of time one spends healing is usually considered. While most cities and *barrios* within cities have someone whom they call upon to prescribe teas and other herbal remedies for minor ills, the curandero is one to whom is brought more serious cases. The curandero does not have another job; healing is the basis of the curandero's livelihood.

In the past, another consideration when measuring the authenticity of a given person's claim to being a curandero was whether that person charged for his or her services. The true curandero was said to take whatever is offered, and there are many recorded instances of curanderos refusing to accept even small payments offered by the very poor. This authenticity measure is no longer applied everywhere. When KPRC-TV in Houston recently prepared a mini-documentary on two modern curanderos, for instance, they found that the youngest, a woman named María, not only charged for her services, but had an hourly rate. "I charge ten dollars for one hour," María boasted. "What I really should be charging is a hundred and fifty dollars an hour…'cause I'm damn good!" María, however, is still the exception.

In many cases, the fact that money is not needed is one reason curanderismo still thrives in Mexican and Mexican-American neighborhoods. Other reasons for its continuity are that there are no language barriers, no need for an appointment and, frequently, no necessity to travel great distances. Moreover, a curandero does not require that patients have medical insurance nor that they fill out complicated forms.

Equally important is the fact that the curandero treats many ailments not even recognized as such by the formal medical establishment. In many cases, these ailments reflect the patient's psychological state. As pointed out by Kiev (1968), curanderismo is a system of medicine which recognizes the profound effect the emotions can have on health. It takes into account the physical manifestations of such feelings as anger, sorrow, shame, rejection, fear, desire, and disillusionment. When one considers that the Western medical tradition has finally begun to recognize the impact of emotions on physical health, the centuries-old practice of curanderismo seems advanced indeed.

What are the attitudes of modern medical practitioners toward curanderismo? Curanderismo was long regarded as superstition or medicine which, at best, treated only imagined ills. More recently, however, the medical establishment has become more tolerant. The holistic movement has done much to promote—for the most part, inadvertently—acceptance of this ancient system. In any case, much writing about curanderismo is addressed to health care professionals and urges them to think of curanderismo as an alternative or a supplement to formal medicine.

Ailments

The most common ailments treated by curanderismo include *susto, caída de mollera, empacho,* and *mal de ojo*—sometimes referred to as *mal ojo,* or just plain *ojo.* Other less frequently encountered ailments, found in Mexico more often than in the United States, include *desasombro, espanto, bilis, muina, latido,* and *mal aire,* sometimes just called *aire.* There are also ills brought about by evil or witchcraft, such as *envidia, mal puesto, salar,* and *maleficio.*

A curandero might be called upon to treat any of the ailments mentioned above. On the other hand, in mild cases, a member of the family might administer an herbal remedy. If the illness persists after a family member attempts to remedy the same, a curandero would likely be consulted. Although definitions of the various ailments and their causes differ, the following are generally accepted.

Although mal de ojo sounds as if it is inflicted through malice, the opposite is the case. Mal de ojo—the evil eye— comes about through excessive admiration, usually of those too weak to absorb it. Babies are the most frequent victims, but animals can contract ojo too. Charms are worn by those susceptible to evil eye. The most common charm is the *ojo de venado* or deer's eye.

Why would admiration cause illness? Some scholars say that it arises from the belief that a person projects something of himself when he admires another. If the person receiving the admiration can't handle it, either because of youth or weakness, illness results. To counteract the effect of the admiration and guard against mal de ojo, the admirer must touch the person, animal, or object of his admiration. The symptoms of ojo are similar to those of colic: irritability, drooping eyes, fever, headache, and vomiting.

Sometimes susto is translated as loss of spirit or even loss of soul. Occasionally, it is translated as shock, although it should not be confused with the life-threatening medical condition known as shock. Receiving bad news can cause susto, as can any frightening event. It is believed that such a scare can temporarily drive the person's spirit or soul from the body. Susto has to be treated immediately or it will lead to a much more serious version, called *susto pasado* or, in Mexico, *susto meco*—an old susto which is much more difficult to treat and which can lead to death.

Weakness is a symptom of susto. Or, as Dolores Latorre describes in *Cooking and Curing with Mexican Herbs* (1977),

"The victim suddenly feels wobbly, chilly, shaky, limp, and drowsy, or he may develop a headache accompanied by nausea." On the other hand, when Ari Kiev describes the symptoms in *Curanderismo: Mexican-American Folk Psychiatry* (1968), he writes that they are "a mixture of anxiety—dyspnea, indigestion, palpitations, and depression—loss of interest in things, irritability, insomnia, and anorexia." Kiev relates one curandero's belief that a susto untreated can lead to heart attack.

Caída de mollera (known as "fallen fontanelle") afflicts only babies. The symptoms are irritability, diarrhea, and vomiting. The baby thus becomes dehydrated and exhibits the most prominent symptom, the one that gives the condition its name: a depressed fontanelle (soft spot). Caída de mollera is thought to be caused by rough handling or from pulling the baby's bottle or the mother's breast from his mouth while he is sucking it. It can also, however, be caused by a fall from the bed or crib, or by the baby himself by sucking too greedily.

The main symptom of empacho is diarrhea and a feeling of weight in the pit of one's stomach. Loss of appetite (not surprisingly) follows. The symptoms of empacho are believed to be produced by something actually stuck in the stomach or blocking the intestines. It can afflict adults, but children are the usual victims.

Empacho is an ailment that reflects the need for balance expressed in the theory of the humors. In brief, it is believed to be caused by improperly mixing hot with cold foods, or eating such foods in improper sequence. Eating too quickly and thus not chewing food completely is another act believed to cause empacho.

As an interesting sidelight, Kiev (1968) points out that both empacho and caída de mollera "are associated with the proper management of children" and are therefore ailments whose presence arouses feelings of guilt in the parents.

Mal aire seems similar to an upper respiratory infection in that it produces earache, stiff neck, chills, dizziness, and headache. What is often called a cold can also be referred to as "aire."

Desasombro is believed to be a more serious form of susto, although it is not to be confused with susto pasado or susto meco, which are more serious because the triggering event or series of events occurred in the past and the ailment was not treated or dealt with. Nor is desasombro as serious as espanto. Desasombro can be thought of as a susto with a more significant cause. If stepping on a snake resulted in a susto, stepping on a poisonous snake would result in desasombro.

Like susto, espanto is a form of spirit loss, but it is much more severe. The difference between the two is explained by Latorre (1977) as follows: "Susto takes place when the victim is in possession of his spirit and, although the spirit may temporarily leave the body due to the fright, the spirit is believed to be nearby and can easily be persuaded to return to the body through the prescribed ritual. Espanto, on the other hand, occurs when a person is asleep. Because at this time the spirit may leave the body to wander far and wide during dreams, it may not be nearby to return into the body when entreated."

Causes of espanto outlined by Latorre include being awakened suddenly by something frightening, such as an intruder, disaster (fire, flood, etc.), a fall from the bed, or by a nightmare.

Bilis is best described as having excessive bile in the system. It is thought to be brought about by suppressed anger. Symptoms include gas, constipation, a pasty-looking tongue, and sour taste in the mouth.

According to Latorre (1977), muína is sometimes called "anger sickness," but it differs from bilis in that it results from a show of rage rather than its suppression. The victim, Latorre writes, "becomes tied up in knots, trembles, and may lose the ability to talk or may become momentarily paralyzed. The jaws may lock, or hearing may stop." Like bilis, muína can result in a discharge of bile throughout the body. Latorre says that it can lead to jaundice.

The symptoms of latido—which translates as "palpitation" or "throb"—were originally a feeling of weakness, and a throbbing, jumpy feeling in the pit of the stomach. At present, however, the term latido is often used to describe a stomach ache. Both forms of latido tend to strike those who are weak and thin.

Some liken latido to a nervous stomach, although others, probably describing the original ailment, say it is like the condition which medical authorities call hypoglycemia. Indeed, latido symptoms usually occur when a person has not eaten for a long period of time.

Envídia, mal puesto, salar, and maleficio are the result of wrongdoing, and most are motivated by envy (or, less often, revenge). The threat of these ailments is often enough to make a person live modestly, never making an obvious show of anything that might inspire jealousy by another. Some of these conditions can be brought about by an individual, but often the individual will engage the services of a witch, or *brujo*, sometimes called a black curandero. Most curanderos, however, are white, that is, they heal in the name of God.

Fortunately, a curandero who is not a witch can remove a hex or spell, and white curanderos are often requested to cure ailments brought about by witchcraft. Or, as happens less frequently, a black curandero can be hired to counter a spell with one of his own.

In one story, a woman reported witnessing the seizure of another woman who was *embrujada* (bewitched). The seizure took place in the presence of the famous Don Pedrito Jaramillo of Falfurrias, Texas. Don Pedrito, according to an account in *The Healer of Los Olmos and Other Mexican Lore* (1975), attempted without success to revive the woman, who had lost consciousness. The woman is said to have awakened, but during another seizure, long after leaving Don Pedrito, she is rumored to have fallen into an open fire where she burned to death.

The famous curandero of Espinazo, Mexico, Niño Fidencio, is said to have left posterity a formula against being hexed. According to Latorre (1977), the formula requires that an aloe vera plant be tied with a red ribbon knotted twelve times and that a lime be attached to the plant with yet another red ribbon. Both should be looped around the aloe vera's roots and then the plant should be suspended upside down above the inside of the front door. In addition, every Friday before sunrise, the plant had to be taken outdoors and placed in water until just before noon. When the plant was brought inside again, the water in which it had soaked was to be sprinkled around the house. Whether this is an effective preventative or simply something to take one's mind off of witchcraft and hexing is not known. These stories do demonstrate, however, that even the most famous of curanderos have had to deal with brujos and the results of their work.

Rituals

While many of the above ailments require that the patient eat, drink, or otherwise use a specific substance, such as an herb, their cures also involve ritual and the use of what an anthropologist would call "symbolic objects." To define the latter, think of the stereotypical view of the "witch doctor" as presented in movies or even comic books: in all likelihood, he wears a mask and carries bones or a rattle. The mask, the bones, and the rattle are clearly symbolic objects, which are supposed to have a certain power in whatever ceremony the witch doctor performs.

A curandera uses symbolic objects as well, such as the cross, pictures of saints, and votive candles. But because she believes her power comes from God, the symbols are shared by many religious people who are not healers. The curandero also uses everyday materials, including olive oil, water, or, most commonly, an egg. María, the modern curandera mentioned above, said that she uses growing plants: "These plants…are very sensitive to their surroundings. When I tell a person that I am going to work on a particular problem for them…if they have an illness of some sort, then what I do is I tell them to buy me a plant. When they buy me a plant, they have automatically put their own vibrations…their own thoughts, feelings… negative and positive…into the plant. The reason a plant works is that once a ritual has been performed where the plant takes on the identity of that person, a spiritual link is formed between that plant and that person. No other person can take on the identity of the plant and vice versa."

Don Pedrito often used mere water, instructing patients to drink, for example, a glass at bedtime each night for a certain number of nights. But the egg figures in most rituals of curanderismo, past and present. Earl Thompson, a novelist of great talent, described one such ritual in *Caldo Largo* (1976): "(The curandera) straightened Lupe's body so she lay face up like a corpse, even crossing her hands on her breasts. As she crossed her hands, she slipped something into Lupe's palms, closed her hands into fists, and told her to hold what she had put in them very tight.

"'What is it?' Lupe asked.

"'Herbs. Now don't talk again until I tell you.'

"The curandera placed candles on the table at Lupe's head and feet. She then poured some fragrant oil from a bottle that had once held tequila into her own large hands, warmed it between her palms and began to work it back through Lupe's hair until her thick reddish tresses were fanned around her face and down over her breasts and body until Lupe gleamed with the oil, all the while chanting some sort of prayer which I could not understand except for the occasional mention of the Mother of Jesus. It was in a dialect I had never heard before. It was hypnotic. I thought Lupe had gone to sleep or fallen into a trance. She seemed hardly to breathe. The smell of the oil was that of jasmine mixed with fresh herbs. The room was very warm and close...

"She massaged Lupe front and back and front again, chanting all the while. The last time she had Lupe hold the egg in her clasped hands on her breast.

"Then she took the egg from her and began gently rubbing it over her forehead, face, neck, and shoulders and then over the rest of her body. She traced the perimeters of Lupe with the egg as if drawing a pattern...

"She then described a cross on her with the egg...[S]he brought the egg to rest finally on Lupe's navel."

Compare the ritual undergone by Lupe to those described by Trotter and Chavira in *Curanderismo* (1981), which was written to provide health care professionals with a better understanding of the subject. Although rituals vary in detail from healer to healer, they have a certain common theme. According to Trotter and Chavira, mal ojo is treated by having "the child lie down and sweeping him three times with an egg. The sweeping is done by forming crosses with the egg on the child's body, starting at the head and going to the feet. While sweeping, the healer recites the Apostles Creed three times, making sure that he sweeps both the front and the back. The egg is cracked and dropped into a glass or jar filled with water. The jar may then be placed on the child's head and another Creed recited. The jar is then placed under the child's bed, usually under the place where the child rests his head. The next morning at sunrise the egg may either be burned or cast away in the form of a cross."

In a book intended for school children entitled, *Discovering Folklore Through Community Resources* (1978), the ritual to cure ojo described by Sumpter is very similar, though less solemn. It is said that in the morning, the egg can either be buried or flushed down the toilet. The egg, once it is broken into the water, is also used for diagnosis: "If the white becomes solid and forms an oval (an eye-shaped ring), people believe that the patient has indeed been suffering from a case of ojo and that he has been cured."

A curandero interviewed by Kiev (1968) said, "You have to break an egg and say a prayer. You break your egg, put it in the glass, and then put some little piece from the broom, you know, on top like a cross, and then the egg starts bubbling. You have to brush (the victim) with the egg first—make like a cross. The egg takes out the evil from the child and makes the person causing it stop...[W]hen the egg starts boiling, that is when you know he had ojo. When the egg goes down, if it does not boil, it means that he doesn't have the ojo."

The ritual of curing susto involves a broom. As described by Trotter and Chavira (1981), "The sick person lies down and is completely covered with a sheet. The healer sweeps the patient with the broom, saying the Apostles Creed three times. At the end of each Creed, the healer whispers in the patient's ear, 'Come, don't stay there.' The patient responds, 'I am coming.' The sick person must perspire and is then given some tea of *yerba anís* to drink. The healer then places a cross of holy palm on the patient's head and asks Almighty God, in the name of the Holy Trinity, to restore the patient's spiritual strength."

The cure for susto which Latorre (1977) describes involves both the broom and the egg: "The cure must be done on three consecutive nights: Wednesday, Thursday, and Friday, the last day being the most effective. The patient lies on the bed with arms extended in the form of a cross while his entire body is cleansed with alum or a whole egg and he is swept with a bundle or broom of herbs, preferably horehound, rosemary, California peppertree, redbrush, or naked-seed weed, tied together or separately. Each evening, fresh herbs are use."

Both rituals involve an invocation to the patient's spirit to return, and the patient's reply. In Trotter and Chavira (1981), the appropriate response is said to be *"Aquí vengo,"* while Latorre (1977) reports that *"Hay voy"* is used. Both may be interpreted as an affirmative response suggesting that the spirit is indeed returning.

Sumpter (1978) reports, as did Latorre, that the cure takes place over a Wednesday, Thursday, and Friday, but shows a curandera first blessing the susto victim's bed with a knife. The healer then sweeps the patient with *cenizo* (pigweed, also known as lambsquarters) and blesses him with holy water. The Apostles Creed is used in this ritual as well, but in addition, the curandera recites from her own personal prayerbook. Only then does she call the spirit, enjoining it to return. After the ritual, the herbs used to sweep the patient are taken home to be placed under the patient's pillow in the form of a cross.

Kiev (1968) describes sweeping too, but the curanderos he interviewed suggested that *granada* leaves be used. One of Kiev's healer informants reported that occasionally massage with an egg was also used for susto.

Don Pedrito, whose cures were often offbeat, is said to have cured a susto by divining what had caused it (the victim had witnessed a murder) and prescribing that a draught of beer be drunk on three successive nights. Still another legend about Don Pedrito is that he once cured a susto by subjecting the victim to another susto: he appeared to the victim in the guise of a bandit to provide the scare (Hudson 1975).

The treatment for caída de mollera is more standardized. As Kiev (1968) reports, "It involves turning the baby over on his heels, pushing up against the roof of the child's mouth, marking the fontanelle area with moist salt, and/or binding the area." Binding the area means smearing it with a sticky substance, usually soap or egg white. It is not uncommon to see babies who have had this area so treated out in public. The thumb is typically used against the roof of the baby's mouth.

An egg can be used to pinpoint the site of the blockage causing empacho. A Mexican American mother interviewed by Kiev (1968), for instance, told of her method of diagnosis: "To treat it, you rub their stomach real good and rub them with an egg at room temperature, not from the fridge...Wherever that egg bursts, that is where the empacho is in the stomach." Massage, followed by the administration of a laxative, is more frequently used. The same woman interviewed by Kiev concludes the description of treatment as follows: "Then they tie a piece of linen around to hold it there. After they do all the rubbing and applying of the egg, they give them a good dose of castor oil or something to make them move their bowels."

Trotter and Chavira (1981) found this combination: "In some cases the healer massages that part of the back behind the stomach with warm oil and pulls on the skin. The skin is said to make a snapping noise when the trapped food particles are loosened. In either case, a tea is given to treat the damaged stomach."

One home remedy is to rub the patient's stomach with shortening and—again, this conveys the notion of loosening something that is stuck—pulling the skin on the patient's back until it pops.

Mal aire is treated like a cold—with tea, lemon juice, even whiskey. Liniments and poultices are used as well.

The treatment for desasombro is much more elaborate, for it is a much more serious illness. One popular treatment outlined in Sumpter (1978) is implemented outdoors at eleven in the morning. It begins when the curandero digs four holes in the ground in the shape of a diamond. One hole is for the head, one for the feet, and two are for the hands. The area is covered with a white sheet, and the patient stretches out, face down, in the form of a cross atop it, with his limbs in the appropriate spots. Another white sheet is placed on the patient. While reciting the Apostles Creed, the curandero sweeps the patient from top to bottom.

It is interesting to note that in various recorded remedies for susto, curanderos have been quite specific about what should be used for the sweeping. For instance, in one case it was granada leaves, and in another, cenizo. The informant for the ritual outlined above says that an ordinary household broom can be used. Thus, rituals can be adapted according to what is available.

In any case, the curandero sweeps the patient and recites the Apostles Creed three times. Now the patient rolls over, face up, hands still outstretched in the form of a cross, and the sweeping ritual is repeated. The patient is now uncovered and stands. The curandero strikes the patient's shadow. Then the curandero drags a piece of clothing which the patient has worn into the patient's house, calling the spirit as he does so. He continues to call until he reaches the patient's bed. The patient comes in, sits on the bed, and drinks a cup of *anís* tea. The patient finishes drinking, leaving a bit of the tea in the cup.

Next the curandero takes some of the dirt that was removed from the four holes he dug when the ritual began. This dirt is mixed with the tea that the patient left. With the resulting mud, the curandero marks the sign of the cross on each of the patient's joints.

The patient then gets under as many covers as it will take to make him sweat. The curandero sweeps the patient now with cenizo and completes the ritual by reciting the Apostles Creed three more times.

Treatment for bilis is far less exotic. Epsom salts or some other laxative would be given once a week for three weeks. On the other hand, the treatment for muína—the other illness caused by anger—is very formulaic. As Latorre (1977) reports: "The affected person is swept with three red flowers on three consecutive days, Wednesday, Thursday, and Friday, and after-ward is given a decoction made with flowers and leaves of the orange tree or other citrus. This will calm the patient. If it does not, the person is struck, shaken, or addressed with un-kind words in order to break the fit of anger." Interestingly, the symptoms which Latorre attributes to muína (provided earlier) are much like those of hysteria. For a long time, and even today, an hysterical person is slapped or shaken, much the same way the victim of muína would be if he didn't respond to the ritual of the flowers.

Latido is usually treated by administering nourishment. Some suggest that a patient take, for nine consecutive days, a mixture of raw egg, salt, pepper, and lemon juice. A more ap-petizing cure requires that the patient eat bean soup with onion, coriander, and garlic. Latorre describes a *comfortativo* made of a hard roll which is split, sprinkled with alcohol, filled with peppermint leaves, nasturtiums, some cinnamon, cloves, and onions. After this is done, the roll is closed, wrapped in white cloth, and bandaged over the pit of the patient's stomach.

The fact is, as farfetched as some of these rituals may sound to readers accustomed to the cold, sterile administration of medical aid, they work! One does not have to believe in the cures in order for them to work. Perhaps most importantly, the curandero focuses his attention one hundred percent on the patient. This undoubtedly is an important component of the healing process. In addition, touch is very important in the healing rituals. Only recently has (a portion of) the medical es-tablishment come to admit the therapeutic importance of touch.

The rituals often involve other members of the patient's family, and many rituals are carried out in the patient's home.

Known as the "curandero of curanderos," Don Pedrito Jaramillo was born in 1829 in Mexico, and died in 1907 at Los Olmos Ranch, north of Falfurrias, Texas. Photograph © Eliseo Torres.

The person who is ill thus has a very deep sense of belonging while the rituals are performed. The status of the curandero also figures in his success. As Kiev (1968) points out, "The curandero is never in doubt as to the diagnosis or treatment and does not undermine confidence in himself among nontechnically oriented patients by ordering laboratory tests and x-rays. He turns to meaningful sources of strength such as the saints and God."

REFERENCES

Hudson, Wilson M. *The Healer of Los Almos and Other Mexican Lore.* Southern Methodist University Press, 1975.

Kiev, Ari. *Curanderismo: Mexican American Folk Psychiatry.* The Free Press, 1968.

Latorre, Dolores L. *Cooking and Curing with Mexican Herbs.* Encino Press, 1977.

Sumpter, Magdalena Benavides. *Discovering Folklore Through Community Resources.* Development and Assessment Center for Bilingual Education, 1978.

Thompson, Earl. *Caldo Largo.* Signet New American Library, 1976.

Torres, Eliseo. *Green Medicine: Traditional Mexican-American Herbal Remedies.* Nieves Press, 1983.

Trotter, Robert T. and Juan Antonio Chavira. *Curanderismo.* University of Georgia Press, 1981.

10

Curanderismo as Holistic Medicine

Gilbert Arizaga, M.D.

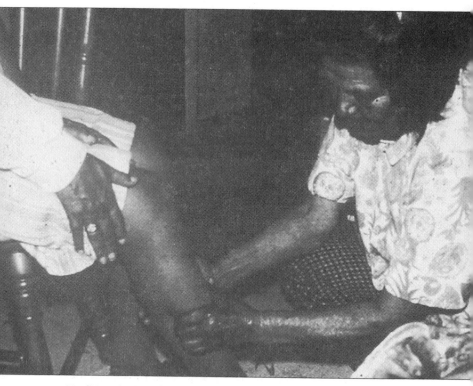

Traditional sobadora *(masseuse) performing massage therapy. Photograph © Eliseo Torres.*

The management of diabetes, or any other medical condition, requires a holistic approach. For some individuals, "holistic" means a natural approach to various treatments, and to some, it means the use of homeopathic medicine. For others, including this writer, it means subscribing to various subtypes of complementary medicine. In fact, agents that might be used to treat a specific medical condition, whether prescription or botanical medicines, are subordinate to and merely a component of a particular healing system.

The initial medical issue, then, is not diagnosing a condition and choosing a medication, but rather identifying and using the healing system available to the patient. If an individual is grounded in a particular culturally relevant system, using treatments specific to the system will be more effective than using "disconnected" treatments. For example, *kava kava*—an herb recently popularized in the United States for the treatment of anxiety—is the nonaddictive botanical counterpart to medications such as Valium. Kava kava, used predominantly in Polynesia within a particular cultural context of community and ritual, is highly effective in promoting a sense of well-being (Norton 1994). In the dominant U.S. culture, however, kava kava used for treating anxiety occurs outside a relevant cultural context, and is consequently less effective.

Because of my Mexican American heritage, I am familiar with the healing system known as *curanderismo*, and have incorporated related concepts into my practice. At present, the Latino population in the United States is rapidly becoming acculturated. On the other hand, *colonias* in the border states and in agricultural regions are undergoing rapid growth. In these population centers and in certain long-settled communities in the Southwest, concepts of curanderismo still exist. Health practitioners must be familiar with concepts of curanderismo if they are to effectively serve Latino populations who are not fully acculturated into the dominant U.S. culture. These Latinos bring with them particular ideas about what constitutes illness. If the physician or counselor does not recognize the importance of this system, the message to the patient is that he or she is irrelevant, and therefore, significant obstacles will be encountered in treatment.

Premises Defining Curanderismo

Curanderismo is syncretic, eclectic, and holistic, because it is comprised of elements from Aztec (Mexica), Greek, Spanish, homeopathic, naturopathic, and modern medicine. It is eclectic because, depending on the clinical situation, one can choose whatever is necessary from the system to invoke a healing process. Curanderismo is holistic because often in disease prevention and always in the healing process, it involves spirit, mind, body, the family, and extended family. The family consists of first- and second-degree relatives. The extended family includes a network of *compadres,* and sometimes friends *(comadres).* Compadres are typically godparents whose relationships are established through spiritual bonds based on Catholic sacraments such as baptism, confirmation, and marriage.

In the curanderismo system, a patient might seek help from a curandero for physiological disorders such as diabetes, psychological conditions such as *susto*, and psychosocial maladjustments such as *mal ojo*. Eight subsets of basic understandings or premises defining curanderismo are discussed below.

(1) ***Mind and body are inseparable.*** Consequently, there is a direct link between emotional and physical symptoms. Some conditions are *bilis* (destructive rage), *susto* (fright), *envídia* (strong envy), and *tristeza* (separation and loss). Bilis, for instance, is a natural disorder in which the patient experiences livid rage with revenge thought processes, and uncontrolled anger induces resentment which becomes self-destructive. Physical symptoms include vomiting, migraine headaches, nightmares, and loss of appetite. Bilis, susto, tristeza, and envídia are believed to be results of an imbalance of "yellow bile."

Examples of the mind-body link are legion. If a diabetic patient experiences a significant emotional stressor, blood sugar may become more difficult to control. If an individual is genetically "atopic," various stressors can be expected to induce symptoms of asthma (wheezing) as well as itching. The itching creates a rash (eczema). Blood vessels can also be very reactive. If they dilate in the skin, hives can develop. If blood vessels are reactive in the intestines, irritable bowel syndrome may develop. Next, if blood vessels are reactive in the brain, symptoms may include migraine headaches. Thus, physical response is dependent on genetic predisposition and psychological or emotional triggers. In some instances, modern medicine confirms the link between emotional and physical symptoms, such as in the research indicating that long-term feelings of hopelessness increase the risk for cardiovascular disease and cancer.

(2) *Balance and harmony are important for well-being; conversely, imbalance produces dysfunction.* Ideas derived from Hippocrates and Spanish priests promoted this concept. Aztec (Mexica) cultural understandings are also incorporated in this premise in the sense that universal opposites, such as hot and cold and good and evil, must be balanced.

The Latino view of healing requires equilibrium between opposite qualities of hot and cold, and moisture and dryness. Disequilibrium results in dysfunction, and dysfunction can develop into disease. In medieval Europe, the body was believed to contain four humors, including blood, phlegm, black bile, and yellow bile. For example, blood was considered to be hot and wet; therefore, bleeding for fevers was deemed logical. Various herbs and foods were prescribed to restore proper balance.

These concepts, cultivated by Hippocrates, are very much alive within the Latino culture. For example, a patient may refuse to take penicillin, considered to be hot, if the disorder is also considered to be hot. Chile, which is hot, is incompatible with exposure to cold night air immediately after a meal. If a child develops chicken pox, he is not to go outside and be exposed to the sun. After a hot shower, it is considered medical anathema to go out in the cold night air.

I recently evaluated a 90-year-old patient and excised a skin cancer from his lip. By definition, excision is considered a "hot" medical event. Accordingly, the patient chose not to consume hot foods as this could impede the healing process and create complications. He explained to his daughters that they must not prepare foods such as refried beans. The daughters seemed perplexed when they discussed the situation with me. Although this is a Latino family, the younger generation did not understand the concept. Similarly, patients in hospitals might ask for *cilantro* (coriander), which is believed to be a "cold" food. For example, a woman who has just given birth to a child (once more a hot condition) would likely not want to eat pork, which is considered to be a hot food. Such a request, of course, could invoke quizzical responses from hospital staff if they are not aware of patients' cultural backgrounds.

(3) *The patient is typically an innocent victim.* Malicious environmental forces—bacteria, witches, evil spirits, or even angry saints—are believed to induce dysfunctions that become internalized, which in turn create disease. However, it is also recognized that the patient's transgressions can induce disequilibrium, thereby creating dysfunction.

Because of the presumed condition of innocence, it is therefore natural for the patient to be surrounded by unconditional love from the church, family, extended family, and friends. Such support provides a platform for the entire family to be involved in the healing process, but does not negate the patient's responsibility to participate as well.

(4) *Body and soul are separable, and both are important.* This premise also defines the importance of the spiritual dimension in curanderismo. Certain forms of susto can be associated not only with common occurrences and causes of fear, but also with separation of the soul from the body, resulting in a sense of loss and depression. Treatment for this condition involves ritualistic prayer rather than poultices and herbs.

Consistent with the idea of separation of body and soul is the belief that the soul can travel in dreams. Belief in the reality of dream travel underlies the notion of facilitating near-death or out-of-body experiences to achieve a positive end. For example, during the Mexican revolutionary period Santa Teresa de Urrea assisted Mexican rebels engaged in combat.

Teresa reportedly laid hands on injured rebels to induce anesthesia. The patient's soul would then travel to various foreign countries, and the patient would experience no pain. Upon completion of the medical procedure, the patient's soul would return to the body. The patient would be fully aware and be able to relate his experiences in the foreign country during his "soul traveling."

(5) *Healing requires family participation and participation by the patient.* Energy flows in both directions as the support and reassurance from the family provides emotional and spiritual energy for the patient to choose to participate in the healing process. Social, emotional, and physical support are critical during times when the patient experiences feelings of hopelessness.

Recently, I evaluated a thirty-year-old Latina woman for stress-induced hair loss. She had lived in a border community all her life, and then recently moved from that community. The stress was the result of the move away from her entire culture, her family, and especially, her mother. I discussed hair loss with the patient from a pathophysiological medical perspective in her cultural context, which included the different emotional issues that must be healed, and that her mother should participate in the healing process.

In the event of "enmeshment," however, family involvement can have negative effects. Enmeshment results in efforts to control the patient, as well as anger and resentment, all of which can interfere with the healing process. Consequently, there are times when a therapist, physician, or curandero must temporarily separate family members in order to isolate problems and help the patient move forward in the healing process. Within the Latino culture, this too must be a family experience.

(6) *The natural and supernatural worlds overlap.* This premise runs parallel to and is closely related to the separation of body and soul. Because the basis of healing is spiritual, prayers, sacrifice, penance, and promises are an important part of curanderismo. In fact, recommendation of prescription or botanical medicines is subordinate to the spiritual, family, and psychosocial aspects of healing.

However, negative spiritual energy can be pathological. For example, in some elements of the culture, it is believed that tissue, such as hair and fingernails, or even clothing that comes into contact with another person can take on the other person's energy. For example, if a young woman wishes to keep her boyfriend, she could obtain his fingernail clippings, grind them up, and keep them with her. In this scenario, the young woman would exert some form of control over him.

(7) *The sick person must be resocialized.* In order for resocialization to occur, the patient must recognize his importance and that he belongs. A mechanism for resocialization is naturally built into curanderismo if the patient chooses to accept it. For example, it is believed that non-Latinos are not vulnerable to folk illnesses such as bilis or susto because they are culturally immune to these conditions. Thus, by merely being diagnosed with one of these disorders, cultural identification exists; although the patient is in disequilibrium, she has a sense of belonging to a community, which provides a foundation for the healing process.

(8) *The healer is expected to interact openly with the patient.* Such interaction is sacred, requiring that the curandero be warm, open, and casual. The curandera in this setting is not an individual who merely performs a ritual, but rather one who has the "gift." Physical contact is important. For ex-

ample, shaking of hands and interacting with the patient are imperative. If a physician is self-absorbed (preoccupied) and does not afford the patient the dignity that he or she deserves, then the Latino patient is completely turned off to the healing process.

According to Maduro (1983), the requirement for participation by the curandera, the patient, and the family is exemplified in the aphorism, *"La vida es una fiesta pero hay que bailar."* (Life is a fiesta, but one has to dance.) In other words, everyone must make good-faith efforts to participate in the healing process, or the dance of life. In the same vein, a fiesta is a communal process, and parallels the communion ritual in Roman Catholicism. This understanding of communion is the outcome of the syncretic nature of Catholicism in Latin America, or the blend of Spanish Catholicism with Indigenous culture. The imperative to become involved underlies Latinos' preference for bargaining in the marketplace. A non-Latino tourist, for example, might wish for a fixed price, but the Latino seller may simply enjoy the process of bargaining prior to the sale.

As described here, curanderismo is a quintessential model for holistic medicine involving spirituality, the mind, the body, family, and community. Usage of prescription or botanical medications is a part of the whole. In the following sections, treatment strategies within the curanderismo healing system for two conditions—mal ojo and diabetes—are presented.

Treatment of Mal Ojo

Mal ojo (evil eye) is one of the more common conditions known to Mexican Americans in the cultural context of curanderismo. This condition has carried negative connotations for some in terms of invoking negative psychic energy. It is believed that certain people can use psychic energy to "communicate" disease to others. In my experience with curanderismo in Grant County, New Mexico, mal ojo is believed to occur when a person, who is presumed to have a strong level of psychic awareness and subconscious etheric energy, has contact with an individual and very much wants to establish a positive relationship with that individual. There is an evident exchange of emotional energy. If the person who initiates the exchange (active individual) does not follow up on the relationship, then medical symptoms develop. For example, the active individual develops severe headaches and the passive individual can experience fever, abdominal discomfort, or diarrhea.

In the case of an infant, the "offender" (initiator) is encouraged to meet the infant, and hold and caress the child. This allows for "laying on of hands" wherein positive energies flow, perhaps through the elevation of natural endorphin and cortisol levels in the body, and the healing process begins. If this does not occur, the infant will develop an illness, and child's family will take him or her to a curandero (or curandera).

Steps in healing within the curanderismo tradition also involve using a combination of herbs that can reduce stomach upset and reduce inflammation and spasms. Combinations of the following herbs are common: *manzanilla* (camomile), *azahar, rosa de castilla* (miracle rose), and *saúco.* These herbs are provided in the form of teas to minimize the potential for dehydration, reduce fever and irritability, and allow healing to begin. Manzanilla is anti-spasmodic and anti-inflammatory. Azahar (flor de naranja) is used for earache, colic, and anxiety. Saúco (*Sambucus canadensis* or elder flower) has been used for facial pain, and for swollen tissue in general, and is also be-lieved to be useful for treating coughs and colds.

Additionally, in an effort to minimize or reduce fever, a fresh egg is placed on the child's body. Placement of the egg has two purposes: the first is to physically absorb heat (and thus negative energy) into the egg, and the second is to sustain the notion that healing comes from the Creator. The egg is con-stantly rubbed on the body in the form of a cross. People in-volved in this process include a curandera, mother and father, close relatives, and frequently members of the extended family and community (compadres and comadres). To further em-phasize the importance of God as the source of healing, prayers are introduced in triplicate, such as in reciting the Our Father, Hail Mary, and Apostles Creed three times each.

Thereafter, the egg which has been used to absorb heat, is cracked open and placed in a small bowl. Because the egg has the appearance of an eye, it reinforces the mal ojo diagnosis. The bowl is placed under the head of the infant's bed, and a simple cross is made from sticks and placed on top of the bowl. The bowl is left under the bed overnight as the praying con-tinues. The egg is then buried outdoors the next day.

It is believed that healing occurs through faith. If faith is fragile or insufficient, then the ritual is repeated for another day, and if necessary, for an additional two days. In some cir-cumstances, a lit candle or a bowl containing holy water is placed nearby. At the end of each ritual, the child's joints are blessed with the holy water.

In summary, mal ojo is induced by psychosocial energies. Healing involves identifying the "offender," and using the cur-andero as a facilitator in a system of healing that involves spirituality, family (including compadres and comadres), and botanical medicines. The curandera is perceived as a person who does not necessarily have to perform specific rituals, but merely as a person who has the *don* or gift (Arizaga 1997).

Treatment of Diabetes

The incidence of diabetes in the United States is estimated at nearly 6%, of which 90 to 95% are Type II (noninsulin dependent), also known as adult-onset diabetes. Prevalence of diabetes among certain groups is higher than for the U.S. population as a whole. For example, 10.6% of all Hispanics have diabetes, compared to African Americans at 10.8%, and Native Americans (persons over 19) at 12.2%. One of the top seven causes of death, Type II diabetes has been linked to lifestyle. For people suffering from this form of diabetes, modifications to lifestyle (diet, exercise, and micronutrient supplements) are often necessary. In addition, the spiritual and cultural base is important in terms of how patients obtain support for and understand the need for lifestyle changes. Moreover, spiritual and cultural support reduces stressors, which lead to or exacerbate diabetes complications.

Control of diabetes treatment is crucial in order to minimize or prevent complications such as diabetic coma, damage to retinas and kidneys, neuropathy (nerve damage), skin ulcers, and poor circulation. For example, guär (leguminous plant high in fiber) and pectin (a water-soluble carbohydrate) supplements have been used successfully. When patients with diabetes eat between 14 and 26 grams of guär per day, they require less insulin. A high-fiber diet also improves all aspects of diabetes control.

A discussion of single nutrients in diabetes is of some

import, although single nutrients should not be the exclusive focus of diabetic control. Sucrose (table sugar) should be minimized as there is evidence that it can elevate cholesterol and triglyceride levels. In addition, sucrose increases platelet stickiness, which can lead to diabetes complications. Chromium supplements are beneficial in terms of enhancing glucose tolerance. There is evidence that diabetes patients with neuropathy suffer from vitamin B^6 deficiency, and thus should take supplements of this single nutrient. Transport of vitamin C into cells is improved by insulin. Thus, dysregulation of insulin can result in a relative vitamin C deficiency, which in turn can contribute to small vessel damage.

Diabetic patients also appear to need larger amounts of vitamin E than nondiabetics. Vitamin E deficiencies result in higher levels of tissue damage in diabetics because of the effects of free radicals. Consequently, vitamin E supplements may help to reduce certain diabetes complications. Next, selenium can assist in the absorption of vitamin E as an antioxidant, and can also reduce platelet stickiness.

Studies of animals indicate that manganese deficiencies can cause increased blood sugar levels. Magnesium deficiency also appears to be present in diabetics, and magnesium levels are lowest in patients with severe retinal damage. Zinc is involved in all levels of insulin processing; consequently, zinc deficiency results in the dysfunction of insulin itself. Zinc supplements are important to diabetics because there is evidence that they excrete excess quantities of zinc. Because the B vitamin biotin works with insulin, biotin supplements are valuable as well.

In addition, various botanical medicines are useful in controlling insulin levels, including onion *(Allium cepa)*, garlic *(Allium sativum)*, green tea *(Camellia sinensis)* and blueberry

(Vaccinium myrtillus) (Pizzorno and Murray 1988:11–12). Garlic has also been useful in the treatment of diabetes in terms of lowering blood sugar, and decreasing platelet stickiness, which reduces the probability of stroke and heart attacks. Onion has similar effects (Pizzorno and Murray 1988). Catechin, the active ingredient in green tea, is also found in *uña de gato*, a popular plant among the Latino population in the Southwest. These plants are anti-inflammatory and beneficial in reducing the development of skin ulcers. Blueberry reduces capillary fragility and leakage, and extracts have been used in Europe for varicose veins. Hypothetically, in combination with gingko biloba, there could be some protection against the development of retinal (macular) degeneration.

REFERENCES

Arizaga, Gilbert, M.D. "Mal Ojo." *The Sundown Cafe Magazine* 1(November 1997):15.

Maduro, Reynaldo. "Curanderismo and Latino Views of Disease and Curing." *The Western Journal of Medicine* 139(December 1983):868–74.

Norton, Scott, M.D. "Kava Demography." *Journal of the American Academy of Dermatology* 31(July 1994):89–97.

Pizzorno, Joseph E. Jr. and Michael T. Murray. *A Textbook of Natural Medicine.* Vol. II. John Bastyr Publications, 1988.

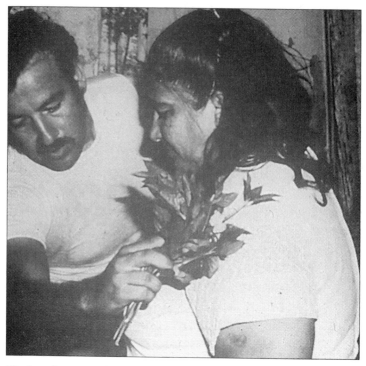

Victim of susto *undergoing spiritual cleansing via sweeping with basil.*
Photograph © Eliseo Torres.

11

Permaculture as a Way of Seeing and Acting in the World

Joel Glanzberg

Intensive potato cultivation in straw bale mulch. This is a labor-saving technique that increases productivity in a small space. Photograph © Joel Glanzberg.

Humanity's technological abilities and ever-increasing detachment from the sources of life have created the illusion that we can invent or manufacture anything we need. Humans are nevertheless profoundly dependent on other beings and natural forces in order to survive and flourish. Permaculture is based on recognition of this interdependence, and could be described as a reintroduction to how the planet we live on really works.

By observing nature we can learn to imitate and work with the features of the landscape and all living things to provide for our own needs, rather than working against natural systems. Permaculture has many applications—by imitating natural systems we can design agricultural systems, buildings, villages, businesses, and even economic systems in ways that are stable, and thereby self-sustaining in the long term. Imitating nature ultimately requires less work than trying to contain or subdue nature because it is like swimming with the current instead of against it.

The "perma" in permaculture represents permanent agriculture and permanence in culture. There can be no permanence in culture without a permanent agriculture, in the sense that a forest or prairie is stable and self-perpetuating, and is thus permanent. Natural systems are self-corrective and thus flexible and complex. Rigidity and simplicity would mean that a particular system is not permanent. Connections, relationships, and attachments are necessary to the establishment and longevity of natural systems, and this is true of any community, whether comprised of plants, animals, or people.

In the remainder of this essay, major principles of perma-culture as a way of seeing (theory) and acting in the world (practice) are discussed. Examples of permaculture in practice in New Mexico and elsewhere are also provided.

All Things Garden

"All things garden" is a central permaculture principle which derives from the fact that all life is based on interrelationship and exchanges among plants and animals. Consequently, all environments are co-created by the plants and animals that inhabit them. In addition, the more exchanges the richer the system, the greater the possible diversity, and the greater the stability of the system.

Consider plant life. When green plants first left the water and began to establish themselves on land, they could not "go it alone." Because plants had not yet added organic matter to minerals, soil did not yet exist. Most of the land was still rock formed from the cooling of molten lava.

Lichens grew on the rocks, as they do today. Lichens are a group of "individual" beings living together symbiotically, meaning that they help one another to survive. They can be comprised of up to fourteen different creatures, but they always contain at least one algae and one fungi.

We are accustomed to seeing algae growing in water, and early on algae in the oceans clung to rocks. Without water, however, algae would have quickly dried out and died. Algae then teamed up with fungi which stored water for the algae.

The algae supplied the fungi with food in the form of sugars produced through photosynthesis. Here we already have a tightly knit community based on exchange and interdependence. This model of cooperation and interdependence is what enabled the great success of biological communities on this planet in every possible niche.

Recently a clear-cut area in Oregon was replanted with seedlings of Douglas fir trees, and all of the seedlings died. An experiment was then conducted wherein seedlings were replanted with a cupful of soil from beneath mature Douglas firs added to the planting hole of each seedling. Ninety percent of the seedlings survived. Why? When the land was clear cut, slash burned, and the surface scraped by machinery and eroded by rain, the soil was effectively sterilized. The first group of seedlings had no help in getting established. The cupful of soil added to the planting holes of the second group of seedlings innoculated them with beneficial bacteria and fungi. These fungi entered the roots of the seedlings and linked them to their own web of root-like mycelia, thereby extending the seedlings' root systems which in turn allowed them access to a larger area of soil and more water and nutrients.

Scientists have found that at least eighty percent of plant families have a symbiotic relationship with a fungi. This should not be surprising given that the first plants on land (the algae in the lichens) depended on one. Though much more complex than lichens, all the plants which surround us today evolved from these simple green flakes on rocks. In a similar way we could not digest our food without the E. coli bacteria which live in our stomachs and intestines.

Next, consider exchanges between animals and plants. All animals (at appropriate population densities) improve their place's ability to provide for their needs. By grazing grass, rabbits encourage tender green shoots. By browsing on shrubs, elk encourage them to resprout multiple, tender growing tips. Birds encourage the seeds of the fruit they eat to sprout: the acid in their stomachs begins to dissolve seed coatings, and then they deposit the seeds far and wide in nutrient-rich bundles. Birds then effectively plant the plants that they live off of as do all fruit- and seed-eating animals. Predators encourage the survival of their prey by culling the herds they live from. Plants improve the soil they live in by dropping leaves, attracting animal droppings, and catching blowing soil and dust. Plants encourage supporting bacteria, fungi, and other plants to grow with them, and they attract animals to propagate them.

As mentioned above, communities or "guilds" of plants and animals have established themselves in every possible biological niche. An example of a low desert guild consists of wolfberry, hackberry, datura, chiltepine, quail, and javelina (or jabelina, wild boar). These plants and animals are interrelated, exchanging something needed for one another's survival.

Another example of a guild involves bluejays, juniper, prickly pear, currants, gooseberries, diverse insects, pack rats, piñons, and quail. A bluejay ate ripe juniper berries one fall. Within her stomach, the seeds were acid treated, and she deposited them in a nutrient bundle while sitting on a rock. The jay was not trying to plant a tree. She planted it simply by being a bluejay. The rain washed the dropping off the rock, and in the moist shade of the rock a tree grew. In time other jays came to eat the juniper tree's berries. From its branches, they dropped packages of seeds they had eaten. In the shaded moist mound of good soil created from the wind-borne debris caught by the juniper, fertilized by its own falling leaves, and enriched by bird and animal droppings, prickly pear, currants, and gooseberries started to grow. While the berries drew more birds, which left their loads of seed- and insect-derived phosphorus, the prickly pears helped to keep large animals at bay. Spreading outward from the tree's canopy, these spiny plants collected and held more soil and nutrients. A pack rat family made its home beneath the plants and hid its winter stash of piñons there. One grew into a tree. In winter, quail shelter in the plants, and fertilize them while planting grasses and eating berries and seeds.

Humans too co-create the environments they live in. When they have a mutually beneficial relationship with their immediate environment, like other animals they improve the capacity of their places to sustain them. On a global scale throughout most of history, human beings interacted with their environments in such a way that they increased their productivity and richness. For instance, when Hernan DeSoto and his soldiers entered what is now South Carolina in 1540, the chronicler of their adventures noted that they "journeyed a full league in garden-like lands where there were many trees, both those which bore fruit and others; and among these trees one could travel on horseback without any difficulty, for they were so far apart that they appeared to have been planted by hand." Careful reconstruction of historic landscape ecology by ethnohistorian Julia Hammett has demonstrated that Southeastern Indigenous tribes managed such landscapes by burning, clearing, and subsequent replanting of useful trees into park-like patches. Similar practices were and still are used worldwide by people to create diverse mosaics of vegetation at varying levels of succession. These practices improved hunting and increased the growth of edible and other useful plants (Henderson and Nabhan 1994:314).

Early Europeans also used such practices, living in beech and oak forests of their own design. When the Romans cleared forests to subdue the Druid insurgency they created feudalism along with barren heaths, warlords, and agricultural peasants. The peasants were required not only to grow food for their own families but also for the nobles, the nobility's armies, and the builders of castles and churches. The peasants used the small "crofts" around their homes very intensively and wisely. They tended highly productive garden/orchards containing many species of plants as well as animals, with whom they also shared their homes.

While the peasantry carefully coaxed as much food, fiber, and medicine as possible from the small amounts of land available to them, and built small, easily heated dwellings, the nobility built large, intimidating structures and purely ornamental landscapes. Versailles, an extreme example of this phenomenon, clearly demonstrates the waste and dysfunction of such landscapes. Little or no thought was given to working with the land—hundreds of hectares—to sustain the people who lived thereon. In this culture, only peasants had to grow their own food. Not only were food plants effectively verboten at Versailles, grounds maintenance requirements for the weed-free paths, clipped hedges, trimmed lawns, and clear-clean pools were extremely high. Cleaning and heating enormous, ornate buildings also required tremendous effort. In the parlance of permaculture, Versailles was an egregious example of "maintained disorder."

Practices such as creating local environments unable to provide for human needs (e.g., where concrete, asphalt, plastic, and grass clippings predominate), while simultaneously degrading environments far from home to meet human needs (e.g., clear-cutting, strip mining, monocropping, and manufacturing that injects toxins in the air, water, and/or soil) are relatively recent, albeit global in scale.

The middle class homes and gardens phenomenon also contributes to maintained disorder worldwide, but particularly in North America and Western Europe. With the rise of the middle class, people sought to imitate the upper classes and abandoned their yard gardens. By the mid-twentieth century, front yards sported manicured lawns, formal walks, and symmetrical plantings of shrubs. If a household had a vegetable garden, it was relegated to the backyard out of sight. As this landscape enslaved its owners (being servantless), it led to a wide variety of manual and motorized lawn tools and lawn care companies.

More water, fertilizer, pesticide, and fuel are used on U.S. lawns than in agriculture. Lawn clippings can feed no one and are often carcinogenic. The uniformity and monotony of these landscapes has led many to yearn for escape. Bill Mollison, a well-known teacher and practitioner of permaculture, once commented when walking through a suburb, "There's no one outside. They must all be inside watching nature programs or off in their four-wheel drive vehicles."

Households and yards can be restored or refashioned to reduce the level of maintenance required, and the use of water, toxic chemicals, and fuel, while simultaneously providing habitat for diverse plants and animals, not to mention food for humans. While development of residential communities is typically destructive, it does not have to be. Part of the promise of permaculture is that when people resume their role as symbionts in natural systems, their residences could help to reclaim damaged and degraded land, while removing pressures from productive lands elsewhere.

In 1986 Roxanne Swentzell and I started to work on a half-acre plot of land at Santa Clara Pueblo, New Mexico. Parts of it had been farmed previously by her grandfather, but most of it was comprised of an extended drive/parking lot. The sandy, dry ground was hardpacked and covered with thorny weeds. Together we completed a passive solar adobe house designed by Roxanne. The house heats itself, and cools itself with the help of a grapevine-covered ramada that shades the west side in the summer. The house includes a passively cooled "refrigerator," and a cold frame which provides winter greens. Roof water runoff and gray water[1] from the house irrigate surrounding gardens.

Windbreaks shelter the house, gardens, and animals. The trees and shrubs provide food for all inhabitants, including the birds that help with pest control, fertilization, and planting. Irrigation water from the *acequia* (irrigation channel) first grows fish in fero-cement water catchment ponds, and then waters food-producing guilds and annual crops. Turkeys convert grasshoppers into meat, while fertilizing the garden. Ducks cull small fish, while fertilizing the algae that the fish eat. Tall locusts shade and protect fruit trees from frost and wind, while currants and gooseberries bear additional fruit under the trees. French sorrel, asparagus, strawberries, and clover carpet the ground. Sheep turn excess greens from the annual vegetable patch into milk, meat, wool, and fertilizer. The wheat grown in the garden is ground on a bicycle-powered mill and baked in an adobe oven fueled with wood from nearby trees. What was once a barren, desertified wasteland is now a highly productive food forest.

Village Homes in Davis, California, has developed a similar pattern at a village scale. Michael Korbit envisioned this residential neighborhood to be both environmentally friendly and pleasant to live in. Houses range from apartment size to single family homes. All buildings are passive solar designs, and some are earth sheltered. All road runoff is caught in large swales and grows large quantities of food crops for the community. Streets are narrow and shaded by trees, thereby reducing summer temperatures. Automobile access is limited, thereby permitting safe use of streets for other purposes. Community gardens add to the productiveness of communal lands. Several people earn a livelihood from products made from surplus garden production. Convenient childcare arrangements and many other benefits have emerged from this integrated community plan. Realtors reportedly hate the Village Homes development because turnover is extremely rare.

Knots in the Flow

In a lecture on patterns in nature, Bill Mollison noted that most people treat everything as trivial. He maintained that in Western culture, everything is seen as individual and separate from everything else, and nothing affects anything else. Consequently, everything becomes trivialized, including ourselves. This mode of thinking underlies people's feelings of impotence, aloneness, and insignificance vis-a-vis the world around them.

Mollison's comments seemed true to me, and it also occurred to me that seeing the patterning in nature is the key to the "permaculture perspective," and the remedy to the isolation he spoke of. As a result of this insight, permaculture no longer seemed to me like a complex system of strategies, ideas, and techniques, but rather, as a way of seeing.

My earliest memories are of the city, where everything was

manufactured by people or at least placed by people. I was surrounded by objects, separate and isolated, capable of existing in any context or none at all. People, including myself, were also insignificant objects, in that all of us were seemingly capable of existing in any context and thus necessary or significant to none. Later, my family moved to the "country," which was on its way to becoming suburbia. Here I was introduced to the woods, which seemed to me like one big life woven out of many.

Around this time I first encountered words that described this feeling or perspective, and they came from Black Elk, an Oglala Sioux holy man: "Then I was standing on the highest mountain of them all, and round about me was the whole hoop of the world. And while I stood there I saw more than I can tell and I understood more than I saw; for I was seeing in a sacred manner the shapes of all things in the spirit, and the shape of all shapes as they must live together like one being. And I saw that the sacred hoop of my people was one of many hoops that made one circle" (in Neihardt 1988).

Black Elk saw all life, made of the hoops of many, including "the two-leggeds, the four-leggeds, the wings of the sky, and all the green things." But how do you make a circle out of hoops? This image or symbol seemed to be referring to a pattern like the one on the back of acorns and pine cones, where intersecting curves weave together to form a circular whole.

Years after encountering Black Elk's words, I gained another piece to the puzzle of understanding from poet Gary Snyder (1980): "[I am reminded] of the Japanese term for song, 'bushi' or 'fushi,' which means a whorl in the grain. It means in English what we call a knot, like a knot in a board...like the grain flows along and then there's a turbulence that whorls...It's an intensification of the flow at a certain point that creates a turbulence of its own...but then the flow continues again. That's parallel to what Black Elk says in *Black Elk Speaks,* talking about the Plains Indian view of physical nature: that the trees, animals, mountains are in some sense turbulence patterns, specific turbulence patterns of the energy flow that manifest themselves temporarily as discrete items, playing specific roles, and then flowing back in again."

Snyder's insight was different from how I was accustomed to viewing the world. I knew that all things are constantly in flux. For example, living things take in material and energy from which to build their bodies and shed waste and dead tissue. Mountains are systems made up of continually accumulating and eroding rock and soil. But I was still accustomed to thinking about these phenomena as "things," whose individuality was primary; nature then would consist of individual things interacting. Snyder, however, suggested that the "things" are merely manifestations of the intersections/knots of flows, not that energy flows occur between or among "things." Rather than seeing the things as primary and the flows as secondary, Snyder transposed the two: energy flows are primary, and all physical phenomena—the manifestations of "knots" in the flow—are secondary.

Patterning in Nature

The face of a sunflower reveals a pattern like those on pine cones and acorns. Two series of logarithmic spirals radiate out from the center. One series curves clockwise and is intersected by the other series curving counterclockwise. When I looked at this one way, it appeared to be a mosaic design created by many seeds of the proper size and shape. But if I looked at it in another way, the flows or curves appeared predominant, with the seeds simply manifestations of the intersections of these flows. The face of the sunflower reflects the patterns of streamline flows in trees and other plants. The sugars, created by sunlight in the leaves, travel to the roots as sap in the phloem. Nutrients and water travel up the plant from the roots to the leaves in the xylem. The patterns they trace are called streamlines. These streamlines connect leaves and roots on opposite sides of the plant (in much the same way as the right and left sides of our bodies are controlled by the opposite hemisphere of our brains). As the exchanges flow between them, they spiral around the center of the plant. They also interweave, changing places. The outer layer of the roots becomes the inner layer of the stem and vice versa. The plant is itself a focus or whorl of flows, twisted and woven together.

Reflections on streamline flows led me to looking at weavings of all sorts, and baskets in particular. When I looked at a Tarahumara basket I saw the sunflower pattern. Again, two series of intersecting curves formed a whole: in this case the curves or flows were obviously primary, and the diamond shapes created by their crossing were (like the sunflower seeds) manifestations of the flows intersecting. Each diamond was a knot where things came together to form "something," and the basket was one big knot, made from many smaller knots.

Once again Black Elk's words came to mind: "...one of many hoops that made one circle." The basket seemed to me like all of nature: a complete whole, made up of intersecting flows held tight by their many strivings to be themselves. I then realized that nature, like the basket, is held together by tension in a dynamic equilibrium. Natural systems are stable then when things are in their right or proper places and interrelationships are not constrained. Instability occurs when interrelationships are constrained or entirely ignored, such as in the maintained disorder of the Sun King's Versailles.

In nature and in permaculture, everything has needs and products. In systems containing or involving humans, any needs not provided by the existing system must be provided by humans. For example, if a building does not effectively heat itself, humans must work to heat it. If an animal is not fed by the surrounding ecological system, humans must feed it. Similarly, if the waste from a building or animal is not used, humans must work to dispose of it, and most becomes pollution without proper handling.

In a permaculture system where things are put in their right places, the chicken, for example, gets to be a chicken (scratching, eating insects, plants, and fruit, defecating, laying eggs, mating, and so on). The chicken's products help humans and the system that supports it. Chicken manure helps to fertilize the plants in the system that feed all system inhabitants. Chicken eggs and young help feed humans, while their scratching controls weeds, pecking controls pests, and their body heat and carbon dioxide warm and enrich winter greenhouse air.

When humans understand that everything around them is alive, and that it is sacred, nothing is trivial. Everything is important. It matters intensely whether you toss that can out or recycle it. It matters intensely whether you use redwood from California or home-grown black locust. Your actions affect everything, and everything affects you. This appreciation of unconstrained interrelationship is a tremendous responsibility, but also a blessing. Human actions are no longer small and meaningless, but important and powerful. The power to "fix" the ecological mess we are in is in our hands. This power does not come from humans being better, stronger, smarter, faster, or more important than something else in the planet's ecosystem. Instead, it comes from humans having a place, and accepting it.

Power is dependent on context. It arises from the symbiosis of combined energy and effort. Human beings function beautifully at their appropriate scale. In fact, the destruction we are trying to heal has been accomplished through countless small acts. This is also how nature heals and builds itself—the accumulation of many small events. Humans too must learn to act in a similar fashion.

We have virtually destroyed the earth's health and its ability to support us by trying to rise above it. It is our responsibility to come down off our high horse to our place, here on the earth. We can only restore health to the earth through nature's own methods. We need to consciously reclaim our place as a part of the system we live in. In the words of Wendell Berry (1994:20–21), "The great obstacle may be not greed but the modern hankering after glamour. A lot of our smartest, most concerned people want to come up with a big solution to a big problem. I don't think that planet-saving, if we take it seriously, can furnish employment to many such people...The health of nature is the primary ground of hope—if we can find the humility and wisdom to accept nature as our teacher."

Conclusion

In the final analysis, permaculture is about deep and abiding respect and reverence. It is about being attached, connected, and belonging. Recent studies in physics, astrophysics, biology, and systems theory indicate that everything in the universe is connected. The cycles of energy to matter and matter to energy, and of birth, death, and rebirth are constant. Our bodies are daily rebuilt while they maintain a coherent order. Humans are like standing waves in a flow of energy and matter. Our form and being persist while what we are made of continually changes. We are inseparable from our surroundings, and our fates are the same. In fact, we are physically attached to people, places, plants, and other animals around us whether or not we are emotionally attached to them.

Permaculture design principles are being used on every continent except Antarctica. From year-round commercial vegetable production in Colorado to community food production for settled tribal members in the Kalahari desert, to city farms in New York, and villages in Cambodia and Vietnam, permaculture principles are being used. Design solutions exist worldwide for every environment and for our technological, social, and economic needs modeled on natural systems.

NOTE

1. Gray water is "used water" derived from bathtubs, showers, and kitchen and bathroom sinks. Black water contains human and animal waste products, and derives from household commodes and collections of livestock waste. It is estimated that the gray water from an average U.S. household could grow all household food requirements, and that the same household's black water would be sufficient to provide for all energy requirements. The latter would require application of technologies to generate biogas and methane, as well as using the "nutrified water" to grow trees used as wood fuel.

REFERENCES

Henderson, Kat and Gary Nabhan. "Gardeners in Eden." In *Restoration Forestry: An International Guide to Sustainable Forestry Practices,* edited by Michael Pilarski. Kivakí Press, 1994.

Mollison, Bill with Reny Mia Slay. *Introduction to Permaculture.* Rev. ed. Ten Speed Press, 1997.

Mollison, Bill. *The Permaculture Book of Ferment & Human Nutrition.* Ten Speed Press, 1997.

_____. *Permaculture: A Designer's Manual.* Rep. ed. Ten Speed Press, 1997.

Neihardt, John G. (preface), Vine Deloria Jr. (introduction). *Black Elk Speaks: Being the Life Story of a Holy Man of the Oglala Sioux.* University of Nebraska Press, 1988.

Snyder, Gary. *The Real Work: Interviews and Talks, 1964–1979.* New Directions, 1980.

12

Renaissance of Ancient Building Practices

A Crucial Element in Restoring Human and Environmental Health

Paula Baker

Mud plaster is applied directly to wall in straw/clay contruction, a "breathing wall" building method. Photograph © Paula Baker, Natural House Building Center.

Until about thirty years ago, indoor air pollution was a very limited phenomenon. Since that time, two basic developments have changed the way that buildings are constructed. First, thousands of chemicals have been incorporated into building materials. Second, buildings are sealed so tightly that the chemicals remain trapped inside, where inhabitants inhale them into the lungs and absorb them into the skin. Prior to the early 1970s, the typical home in North America averaged approximately one air exchange per hour. Now, in a well-sealed home, the air is typically exchanged as little as once every five hours or longer, and that is not enough to ensure healthful air quality.

Of the more than 80,000 chemicals common in commercial use today, less than 1,000 have been tested for toxic effects on the human nervous system. Furthermore, the use of chemicals known to be harmful is rarely restricted. The cumulative and synergistic effects of numerous chemicals simultaneously interacting in a closed environment have never been adequately studied. That new building (and car) smell that we are familiar with is the aroma of chemical soup! People everywhere in formal and informal studies are writing and talking about the impacts on the human species, and thousands of animal and plant species, resulting from the last fifty years of chemical exposure. Practically every living organism, as well as the air, soil, and waterways throughout the world have been subjected to a massive unregulated experiment called "better living through chemistry."

Creating healthy buildings has now become a matter of professional ethics for some architects and builders. Using toxic materials in building construction is destructive to the planet, construction workers, workers involved in the manufacture of materials, and the people living and working in the buildings. In order to truly nurture human beings, buildings must not only be beautiful in a spatial sense, they must also be healthful and conceived with mindfulness of place as well as natural resource sustainability. The same building can be destructive of human health and the environment, or enhance human vitality with zero impact on the environment. The difference lies in the materials and methods of construction.

Approaches to Healthy Building Practices

There are two basic trends in healthy building. Both schools of thought strive to eliminate the use of toxic building materials. However, they are fundamentally different in their basic philosophies.

High Tech

The high-tech approach is to eliminate as many pollutants as possible from the construction process and to create an energy efficient and well-sealed interior filled with mechanically vented and purified air. A high-tech oasis is created, separating the inhabitant from a hostile environment. For many who have become highly chemically sensitive, even the natural world has become an unsafe environment. Wood turpenes and aromatics found in natural building products can elicit symptoms as severe as those caused by manufactured pollutants. For people facing severe multiple chemical sensitivities, a sealed environment may be the only effective means of creating a safe haven.

Baubiology

Whereas separation and impermeability are the operative concepts for the first school of healthy building, interaction and permeability are the key concepts of the second philosophy known as baubiology (or *bau-biologie* in Europe). Baubiology is the study of how buildings affect human health. According to baubiology, the building envelope is viewed as a third skin, with people's clothes as the second skin. It is seen as an organism interacting with the surrounding natural world and facilitating a balanced exchange of air and humidity.

Bau-biologie is a household word throughout much of northern Europe, but it is still an unfamiliar and strange sounding term to most people in North America. I have come to embrace the principles of baubiology in my work as an architect because it offers a holistic approach to building, and bridges the gap between two major environmental movements that have often operated at cross purposes to one another. I believe that people dedicated to energy efficiency and environmental sustainability and restoration must also look "inward," that is, toward the creation of indoor air quality that sustains individual human beings' health and vitality. And people dedicated to creating healthful and nurturing indoor environments must also consider the larger environmental picture and the health of the planet's entire ecosystem.

Baubiology incorporates numerous basic principles for creating healthy environments, and the use of nontoxic materials is just one of them. Several of these principles deal with more subtle aspects of human health, taking into account the spiritual and psychological factors that contribute to human well-being. Some of the most important principles are summarized below.

Consideration of site geobiology and preservation of natural magnetic fields. Many Indigenous peoples have traditions for finding the proper sites for dwellings, as well as healthful orientation, placement of openings, and structural design. In the same vein, baubiologists' studies show an increased incidence of health problems, including insomnia, cancer and other immune disorders, among people living in areas where the earth's natural electromagnetic fields are disturbed or intensified. It is especially important to avoid sleeping over these "geopathic zones."

Incorporation of natural light, illumination, and color. In the past in the United States many hospital walls were painted "hospital green" because green walls were believed to have a healing and calming effect on patients. With this exception, color theory has received little attention in mainstream architecture. However, baubiology focuses in depth on the effects of natural light, illumination, and color on people's mental, physical, and spiritual health and well-being, and suggests practices for enhancing all three.

Architectural proportion and harmonic order of space. There is a famous adage about modern architecture that "form follows function." However, Indigenous peoples had a much less anthropocentric view of the world, and it might be said in these cases that form reflects cosmology. The ancient Chinese art of placement, *feng shui,* harmonic proportions based on the "golden mean" used by the Greeks, the Navajo hogan, and

West African dogon huts, are all examples of architectural forms that traditionally have sought to embody far more than mere human function.

Minimization of manufactured electromagnetic fields. The presence of electrical and magnetic fields, although invisible to the naked eye, are quantitatively measurable by simple instrumentation. There have been many contradictory and controversial studies of their effects on human health. Sweden and a handful of other nations have established safe exposure limits. The U.S. government advises "prudent avoidance," but has set no standards on the amounts of exposure that would be prudent to avoid.

There are several simple measures that anyone can take to reduce exposure to electromagnetic fields. For example, a gauss meter is a simple instrument used to measure magnetic fields; one can quickly determine where a field created by motorized equipment falls to an insignificant level. A gauss meter can also detect electrical wiring errors that cause net current. (Net current from wiring violations is another common cause of magnetic field exposure.)

The effects on humans and other living organisms of alternating electrical current has been well studied by baubiologists, but almost completely ignored in mainstream building science. Experts in the field agree that sleeping in a neutral field is very important. Whether one is building a new structure or simply retrofitting an existing bedroom, there are many simple strategies for creating an "oasis" free of electromagnetism.

Respect for living arrangements of families and the larger community. In many cultures, there is a tradition of passing homes on from generation to generation. The same buildings have been lovingly restored and altered for hundreds of years.

This is not common in North America, where the average person moves several times over the course of a lifetime, and buildings are not conceived of with the legacy of great grand-children in mind. As a result, dwellings are considered to be more of an investment commodity than a family heirloom. Initial cost per square foot rather than life cycle costs tend to be the driving force behind the materials chosen for housing. Because building materials have become less and less substantial, it has become cheaper to tear down and build anew than to restore. Not only is this an ecological travesty, but it is a cultural one as well as we constantly tear away at the physical fabric of our collective history.

Other principles of baubiology address the issues of environmental health on a global scale.

Use of natural and local materials that are renewable and low in embodied energy, and avoidance of materials manufactured through the exploitation of the environment or other human beings. An important emphasis in baubiology is a "cradle to grave" analysis of building materials. What is the real cost of a product or material used in building? Where was it harvested in its raw form? Was ecological harm done in extracting it? Was a community damaged as a result of extraction? How much energy went into its manufacture? Did a factory manufacturing the material issue pollution and therefore harm workers and/or the surrounding community? Were workers treated fairly or exploited? How far did the material have to be transported to get it to the building site? Will it emit toxic fumes during the life of the building? When the building is finally abandoned, will this material return gracefully to the earth, or will it pollute soil and water in a landfill for hundreds or thousands of years?

The total picture of the life cycle of a product determines the amount of "embodied energy" inherent in a building material. Materials that are locally found and unprocessed have the lowest embodied energy, and therefore tend to be the most ecologically sound choices. If Eskimos can build homes of mainly water, imagine how rich the palettes are for most inhabitants of North America by comparison. All Indigenous peoples have found ingenious and elegant ways of creating dwellings with materials found in a very limited radius.

Use of energy-efficient materials and building systems. There are many simple measures that can be used to increase the energy efficiency of dwellings. By paying attention to such measures, we can decrease energy costs and pollution while increasing comfort. A sampling of such measures includes solar orientation, planting of deciduous trees and shrubs for natural summertime cooling and winter heating, proper orientation of openings and structures for cross ventilation, use of highly insulated exterior wall materials, and massive interior wall construction.

Use of solar energy and radiant heat sources. Solar energy is nonpolluting, nontoxic, and nonexploitative in its production and, in a commercial sense, is free for the taking. Heat from the sun is one form of radiant heating. Others include wood stoves, radiators, and baseboard and radiant floor heat. Whereas forced air heats the air, radiant heat sources heat objects, including people, and therefore provide a higher degree of comfort. Constant temperature and instantaneous control of temperature within a dwelling are rather recent expectations in the history of humankind. Baubiologists argue that this "comfort addiction" runs contrary to best interests of human health and that people consume far more energy than necessary to "feed" their habitats.

"Breathing Wall" Building Methods

In recent years several ancient methods of building have been revived which use natural, locally available materials such as earth, clay, sand, and straw. The use of these methods can fulfill most, if not all, baubiology principles mentioned above. Brief descriptions of these methods are provided below. (Sources for details on all methods, including drawings and instructions on material contents and construction, can be obtained in the References section.)

Each of the following methods has great potential for healthy house building because the walls themselves provide insulation and they can be finished with a covering of plaster applied directly to the wall. The need for exterior sheathing, batt insulation, gypboard, joint fillers, and paint is eliminated. Many volatile organic compound (VOC) contamination sources are thereby eliminated as well. Because the walls are porous and interactive with the natural environment, temperature and moisture levels are modified and a slow exchange of air through the wall material takes place. This concept, known as a "breathing wall," is one of the basic principles of baubiology. Because all such methods use locally harvested and renewable resources, impact on the environment is minimal compared to methods based on manufactured materials.

Adobe

In the U.S. Southwest, adobe has long been a common building material, and predates building codes. Because the R-value of adobe is fairly low, it requires additional insulation in order to meet state energy requirements in all but the warmest portions of North America. (R-value, a measurement of thermal insulation, indicates resistance to heat flow. The U.S. Department of Energy has recommended R-values for every area of the United States. Higher R-values are recommended for colder climates.) A higher R-value is usually obtained by adding foam insulation to the exterior of the building which affects the "breathability" of the wall and marries an environmentally friendly product to an unfriendly one.

Adobe blocks are frequently "stabilized." One of the main reasons for this procedure is to prevent breakage during transport. The most common stabilizer is asphalt, a material that should be avoided in a healthy home. Unstabilized adobe can be purchased from some adobe yards. Adobe blocks can also be made on site with an adobe press, thereby obviating the need for stabilizers.

Cob

Cob was a traditional form of building throughout preindustrial Europe, and can easily be used for sculptural shapes. It has recently been revived in the United States by The Cob Cottage Company. A mixture of moistened earth containing suitable clay and sand content is combined with straw and formed into loaves which are then piled onto a wall and blended with previous layers. The result is a monolithic, load-bearing mud wall. At least 18" thick, the wall can serve as an insulating wall with no need for foam insulation and stabilizers. The cob method is time consuming, but does not require a high degree of skill or specialized tools.

Rammed Earth

Earth containing the proper moisture and clay content is rammed into formwork in 6" to 8" layers. The walls are thick, precise, and beautiful. Different colors of earth can be used to create decorative effects. The walls do not require plaster or further insulation. This technique is most suitable in arid climates. In earthquake zones, steel reinforcement may be required.

Straw Bale

A large amount of information is currently available about straw bale construction due to its renaissance as a building material. Its thick, highly insulated walls are extremely energy efficient and beautiful. Several states including California, New Mexico, and Arizona issue building permits for straw bale construction. This new development is the work of a few dedicated individuals who have spearheaded efforts to perform stringent fire and structural testing. These expensive tests are required for code approval. Whereas some states will permit load-bearing straw bale construction, others will permit it only as infill material between a post and beam structure.

Because much of the straw grown in the United States is heavily sprayed with pesticides, locating organically grown straw is recommended. Another feature to be aware of is that bales of straw often contain mold. Because the walls are allowed to breathe, in theory the bales will always remain dry enough so that mold will not be a problem. However, should water become trapped in the wall due to roof failure, plumbing leaks, poor drainage or other building systems failures, then ambient mold can become a problem. As with most building systems, water and moisture management strategies must be incorporated in the design in order to prevent mold growth.

Straw/Clay

Straw/clay construction combines the mass of adobe with the insulating capacity of straw. Straw is mixed with a clay soup and rammed into forms. This is an ancient European method of building that has only recently been introduced in the United States. The technique uses straw clay as an "outstanding" wall around timberframe structures. The result is a precise wall that can accept mud plaster without any further wall preparation.

Pumicecrete

In this method, thick walls are created by mixing pumice, a very porous volcanic rock, with a light soupy concrete. The mixture is poured into formwork. The resulting walls have both thermal mass and a high insulation value, and are ready to accept plaster without further preparation.

Summary

When planning to build with any of the above breathing wall materials, careful inquiry must be made into permit status with local building authorities. Regional factors such as drainage, rainfall, temperature, humidity, freeze and thaw cycles, and the availability of natural materials will make some of these solutions more suitable in certain locations than in others.

REFERENCES

Baker, Paula, Erica Elliott, and John Banta. *Prescriptions for a Healthy House: A Practical Guide for Architects, Builders, and Homeowners.* InWord Press, 1998.

Cob Cottage Company. *Earth Building and Cob Revival: A Reader.* 3d ed. Cottage Grove, Oregon: Cob Cottage Company, 1996.

Easton, David. *The Rammed Earth House.* Chelsea Green Publishing Company, 1996.

King, Bruce and Ann Edminister. *Buildings of Earth and Straw: Structural Design for Rammed Earth and Straw Bale Architecture.* Chelsea Green Publishing Company, 1997.

Laporte, Robert. *Mooseprints: A Holistic Home Building Guide.* Santa Fe, New Mexico: Natural House Building Company, 1993.

MacDonald, S.O., and Matt Myhrman. *Build It With Bales: A Step-by-Step Guide to Straw Bale Construction.* Version 2. Chelsea Green Publishing Company, 1998.

McHenry, Paul G. *Adobe: Build It Yourself.* University of Arizona Press, 1985.

_____. *The Adobe Story: A Global Treasure.* University of New Mexico Press, 1998.

Roodman, David Malin, and Nicholas K. Lenssen. *A Building Revolution: How Ecology and Health Concerns Are Transforming Construction.* Washington, D.C.: Worldwatch Paper 124, March 1995.

Steen, Athena Swentzell, Bill Steen, and David Bainbridge. *The Straw Bale House.* Chelsea Green Publishing, 1994.

13

Natural Foods Retailers as Activists for Sustainable Lifestyles

John Macker

Fresh produce market at Wild Oats in Santa Fe, New Mexico. Photograph © John Macker.

The health food industry has been growing by leaps and bounds, largely because it originated as a response to people's needs. Concerns about "natural foods" surfaced in the context of the environmental movement and counter-culture of the 1960s. People wanted to avoid eating foods laced with preservatives and other chemicals, as well as to prevent contamination of the planet's water, soil, and air for purposes of improved health for individuals and the ecosystems they are a part of. This dual focus was an extension of the era's social justice movements. From the 1960s to the present, people who frequent organic foods retail outlets tend to have adopted an integrated lifestyle which encompasses liberal politics, opposition to war-making and nuclear testing, commitment to environmental preservation and restoration, biological diversity (e.g., reintroduction of endangered predator species, creating and developing seed banks), and so on. In brief, these people are not coming in simply to buy an herb to feel better.

In the late 1990s, organic and natural foods and herbal remedies are often found on store shelves of large supermarket chains. Prior to the "mainstreaming" of many such items, natural foods retailing was concentrated in small, independently-operated stores in upper middle-class suburbs, college towns, and upscale urban areas. Greater availability of healthy foods and supplements (sometimes at lower prices) is beneficial to consumers, while presenting economic challenges to retailers specialized in organic products. At present, there are at least two natural foods retail chains operating across the country, and innumerable, smaller operations vying for the health-conscious consumer dollar.

Specialty natural foods retailers will continue to be viable, and even vital, parts of their respective communities into the foreseeable future as long as these businesses continue to fulfill needs and expand in the following interdependent areas: (1) provide information on the benefits of organically-grown, natural foods, and on the benefits and usage of herbal and homeopathic remedies, and (2) serve as a catalyst and resource for diverse grassroots campaigns aimed at improving the health of the natural environment and its inhabitants. These roles and activities of natural food retailers are discussed in detail below.

Interaction with Community

The philosophy of retailers such as organic food stores should be one of helping to sustain and revitalize the surrounding community. The intent here is to achieve a "balance of benefits," that is, the store gives back to the community which sustains it. There are many levels and ways of providing benefits to the community. A few of the most basic are listed below.

Employ local people at decent wages, including herbalists and nutritionists. The larger stores employ up to 150 full-time local people working in cashier, juice bar, deli, natural living, customer service, grocery, and produce positions. Employees also engage in outreach to schools, such as giving lectures and workshops on nutrition.

Become an extension of the community. This commitment is increasingly reflected in the layout of natural foods stores as well as the air quality inside the stores. For instance, in two local stores, there is space dedicated to purchasing food products; a cafe area for snacking, chatting, and reading; an area dedicated to books and sundry items; a place to make local phone calls; a community bulletin board; a massage area where a therapist is on duty several hours a day; and more. Moreover, the entire premises are "safe zones" for people with environmental illnesses and special diets. These layouts were based on an "organic model," which is intended to give people a place that feels like a neighborhood, in that people want to be there and feel comfortable. The local health foods store should provide networking and be a viable resource tool for issues of community, regional, and national interest, as well as set up recycling receptacles and educate people about recycling.

Nurture nonprofit organizations. A health food store's philosophy and priorities should be directly reflected in the nonprofit company it keeps. Much of a retailer's energy and resources can be directed toward "green" groups such as the Sierra Club, Forest Guardians, Amigos Bravos, and countless other smaller organizations dedicated to environmental preservation and restoration. These relationships are truly sustainable and symbiotic as they represent cultural ecology at its most activist and effective.

All nonprofits supported by a health food retailer should, for example, advocate environmentally sustainable agriculture and lifestyles, prohibitions against animal testing and cruelty, and the like. The retailer can participate in these organizations in numerous ways, including sponsorships, cash or gift certificates, and product donations. The Wild Oats store in Santa Fe, New Mexico, for instance, has participated in health and fitness fairs, AIDS-related walks and fundraisers, five- and ten-kilometer runs, bike races, and tournaments for diverse non-profits; school sports sponsorships; and cooking programs in schools. Store space is also available for nonprofit tabling, raffles, fundraiser sales, and so forth. In turn, the community can recognize the "kindred spirit" of the store as it promotes its own organics, cruelty-free body care products, hormone- and anti-biotic-free meats, and "clean" dairy and other food products.

Develop community education programs. You simply can't put up a store with a sign saying, "Get your organic foods here," and expect people to flock to your doors. For example, what does "organic" or "sustainable agriculture" mean? Much arcane knowledge, such as in the case of herbs, has not yet be-come mainstream. The consumer should be able to find out how much echinacea he or she should take, as well as the latest information on wolf reintroduction in the Southwest, for ex-ample. The objective here is educated consumerism, buttressed by expanded social consciousness and environmental aware-ness based on information, ancient and brand new. In local natural foods stores, classes and other educational forums on topics ranging from herbal laxatives to peri-menopause are welcomed by consumers. Cooking classes are offered ranging from the vegetarian to the exotic, as are lectures on diets, hypnotherapy, Viking history, the world of teas, herbal medicine making, drumming, children's holiday crafts making, chronic back pain, and much more. Knowledgeable, enthusi-astic, and compassionate employees (who are ideally involved with their communities in their own ways) are available to guide (and reassure) the consumer.

Celebrate the earth, Indigenous agriculture, local growers and food traditions. A successful health food store concerned with promoting human and environmental health and cultural dynamism of its community can be an essential link in the cultural/ecological chain that begins with a celebration of the earth. The earth sustains native plants, grown and harvested by the Indigenous people of the area. Local products can be purchased by the retailer and sold to the consumer as "locally, organically grown produce."

Many natural foods stores are attempting to help farmers stay on the land, and reaching out to local growers is essential. There are certain times of the year when it is more feasible than others to bring in local fresh produce. The consumer should be able to shop and be assured that local vendors, growers, and manufacturers are well represented, alongside national brands, and that free samples of foods are available every day in all departments.

Toward a Sustainable Eco-Economy

At this time in history, organic food retailers must become examples for other businesses to emulate, and this includes the positions they take on issues of national and global importance. Certain national campaigns underway at the time of this writing are described below.

Demand that irradiated foods continue to be labeled. As of early 1999, the U.S. Food and Drug Administration (FDA) began soliciting public comment about whether changes are needed for federal regulations requiring irradiated food to be labeled as such. The FDA was considering less conspicuous labeling, such as irradiation being included as part of a list of ingredients. Organic food retailers insist that irradiation labeling remain obvious and overt in order to provide shoppers with a clear choice between products. According to surveys, a large majority of the U.S. public does not want to eat irradiated foods, and with good reason. Organic food retailers assert that radiation destroys the nutritional value in foods and creates waste products that cannot be disposed of in an environmentally sustainable fashion.

Insist that organic food standards are rigorous and coherent. The Save Organic Standards (SOS) campaign was part of a national effort in 1998 to oppose national standards for organic food proposed by the U.S. Department of Agriculture (USDA). That effort resulted in over 275,000 comments to the agency and forced the USDA to back off on several key issues, including genetic engineering, food irradiation, and the use of sewage sludge in the production of organic foods. In October 1998, the USDA published three issue papers, and gave citizens until December 15 to submit comments. The issue papers covered only a portion of the larger proposed federal regulations on organic standards, dealing specifically with (1) animal confinement, (2) animal antibiotics and medications, and (3) procedures for terminating or decertifying organic producer certifications. Once again, the USDA was deluged with comments expressing strong opposition to USDA proposals.

At the time of this writing, the USDA is working on a second set of proposed federal regulations on organic standards to be published later in 1999. Meanwhile, a variety of organic food retailers and other organizations are developing a strategy that will ensure strong organic standards no matter what the USDA does. One national organic food chain has launched a campaign for ensuring that every single ingredient in a product would be accounted for. All ingredients and their respective acceptable or unacceptable "status" would be listed onpause are welcomed

Vociferously oppose distribution of "terminator technology." Monsanto Corporation recently acquired a patent on plant genes that render plants sterile. Consequently, farmers could not retain a portion of their harvests to use as seed. Instead they would be forced to return to Monsanto, paying whatever the company demands before they could plant the next season's crop. As articulated by environmentalists and many organic foods retailers, this technology is pathological: it's a question of who controls the seeds of life.

Conclusion

Organic food retailers are not islands: although we cannot please everyone all of the time, we must make an effort to please most people most of the time. Our most fundamental objective is to participate in creating and maintaining a sustainable community. In a sustainable community, people take care of the land and of each other. Toward achieving this objective, we are committed to empowering people through helping them achieve a healthier lifestyle and a positive vision of the future.

Indian corn and gourds. Photograph © Marcia Keegan.

Contributors

Gilbert Arizaga, M.D., a native of southwestern New Mexico, is board certified in pediatrics and dermatology. One of his major interests in dermatology is psychocutaneous medicine, that is, utilizing the skin as a window for the evaluation of internal stressors. He presently practices dermatology in Silver City, New Mexico.

Kenny Ausubel has founded or cofounded Seeds of Change, Inc., the annual Bioneers Conference, and the Collective Heritage Institute, all concerned with one or more elements of preserving biodiversity, cultural diversity, traditional farming practices, and developing alternative farming strategies. He is author of *Seeds of Change: The Living Treasure* (HarperCollins, 1995), an account of the biodiversity preservation and seed saving work of Seeds of Change, Inc., and "Restoring the Earth: Visionary Solutions from the Bioneers," a film which profiles heroic environmental innovators with pragmatic solutions for instituting widespread environmental improvement. Kenny is also founder of Inner Tan Productions, a feature film development company devoted to social issue projects. He produced, wrote, and directed the documentary film, "Hoxsey: How Healing Becomes a Crime."

Paula Baker, AIA, is an architect and baubiologist intimately familiar with the materials and methods of standard construction, and where they are in conflict with human health. She has identified and employed alternatives to standard materials and methods for several years. Paula is the founder of Baker and Associates in Santa Fe, New Mexico.

Brett Bakker, New Mexico field manager for Native Seeds/ SEARCH, has also spent time with the San Juan Pueblo Agriculture Project, Plants of the Southwest, Flowering Tree Permaculture Institute, New Mexico Organic Commodity Commission, Talavaya Seed Company, and the University of New Mexico. Since 1977, he has worked with native and heirloom seeds as a farmer, collector, seed bank tech, and nurseryman. A most enjoyable part of his work is being fed on reservations throughout New Mexico.

Clayton Brascoupe, a Mohawk of the Iroquois Six Nations, raises organic foods and uses traditional Native American methods whenever possible on his farm at the Tesuque Pueblo in northern New Mexico. He has worked in agriculture in many regions, beginning in the Iroquois Six Nations country.

Gregory Cajete, Ph.D., a Tewa Indian from Santa Clara Pueblo, New Mexico, is an assistant professor in the College of Education, University of New Mexico, and author of *Look to the Mountain: An Ecology of Indigenous Education* (Kivakí Press, 1994) and *Ignite the Sparkle: An Indigenous Science Education Model* (Kivakí Press, 1999). He has been a New Mexico humanities scholar in the ethnobotany of northern New Mexico and a member of the New Mexico Arts Commission. Gregory has lectured at a number of universities nationally and in Canada, Russia, Japan, and New Zealand. He is the former chair of Cultural Studies and dean of the Center for Research and Cultural Exchange at the Institute of American Indian Arts in Santa Fe, New Mexico.

Yvonne Dion-Buffalo, Ph.D., is involved in research and activism surrounding cultural traditions of nutrition, agriculture, and ecology of Indigenous peoples. At present, she is a post-doctoral fellow in the Department of Anthropology, State University of New York at Buffalo.

Joel Glanzberg has been applying and teaching permaculture in the Southwest for over ten years. He cofounded Flowering Tree Permaculture Institute with Roxanne Swentzell and Brett Bakker in 1986 to study traditional Southwestern lifeways and their applications in permaculture. His work has focused on agricultural, architectural, and handcraft aspects of permaculture. For ten years, his work revolved around the development of Family Tree, a family-based permaculture demonstration and experiment site at Santa Clara Pueblo, New Mexico. This work has been featured in "The New Garden" television show and *The American Gardener* magazine. Joel is a carpenter and blacksmith, as well as a respected teacher and consultant in land use.

John Macker is a poet and journalist who has lived in Colorado and northern New Mexico for twenty years. His latest book of poems is *Burroughs at Santo Domingo* (Denver: Long Road Press, 1998). While residing in Colorado, John edited the award-winning arts magazine *HARP* from 1991 to 1995. He has been involved in the marketing side of the whole foods industry for several years.

John Mohawk, Ph.D., a Seneca of the Iroquois Six Nations, is an associate professor in the American Studies department, State University of New York at Buffalo. He is former editor of the *Akwesasne Notes*, cofounder of the Daybreak Farming and Food Project, and author of *Utopian Legacies: A History of Con-*

quest and Oppression in the Western World (Clear Light Publishers, 1999). John has been a farmer for twenty-five years.

Enrique Salmón learned from his Rarámuri (Tarahumara) mother and grandparents how to harness the medicinal, nutritional, and spiritual value of plants. It was only natural for him to pursue a career in ethnobotany and apply what he had learned. A result of this path is the Baca Institute of Ethnobotany (in Durango, Colorado), which Enrique founded. The Baca Institute is the first independent nonprofit dedicated to ethnobotanical education, research, and scholarship of the medicinal and food plants of the Indigenous peoples of the southwestern United States and northern Mexico. Enrique has a B.S. from Western New Mexico University, an MAT in Southwestern Studies from Colorado College, and is currently a Ph.D. candidate in anthropology, linguistics, and botany at Arizona State University.

Lawrence Shorty is a Navajo currently working toward his doctorate in health education at the University of New Mexico, Albuquerque, New Mexico.

Eliseo Torres, Ph.D., received his doctorate from Texas A&M University-Kingsville, and did postgraduate work at Harvard University. He is currently vice president of student affairs at the University of New Mexico. He is the author of two books, *Green Medicine: Traditional Mexican-American Herbal Remedies* (Nieves Press, 1983) and *The Folk Healer: The Mexican-American Tradition of Curanderismo*. Eliseo is also a recipient of the Martin de la Cruz Medal, an award bestowed to practitioners, researchers, and others who have contributed to the advancement of traditional and folk medicine, by the Academia Mexicana de Medicina Tradicional.

Further Reading

Badshah, Akhtar A. *Our Urban Future: New Paradigms for Equity and Sustainability.* Prometheus, 1996.

Bernard, Ted and Jora M. Young. *The Ecology of Hope: Communities Collaborate for Sustainability.* New Society Publishers, 1996.

Blackburn, Thomas C. and Kat Anderson. *Before the Wilderness: Environmental Management by Native Californians.* Ballena Press, 1993.

Caduto, M.J. and J. Bruchac. *Keepers of the Earth.* Fulcrum Publishing, 1988.

_____. *Native American Gardening.* Fulcrum Publishing, 1996.

Cajete, Gregory A. *Look to the Mountain: An Ecology of Indigenous Education.* Kivakí Press, 1994.

_____. *Ignite the Sparkle: An Indigenous Science Education Model.* Kivakí Press, 1999.

Caulfield, Richard A. *Greenlanders, Whales, and Whaling: Sustainability and Self-Determination in the Arctic.* Dartmouth College, 1997.

Cobb, John B. Jr. *Sustainability: Economics, Ecology, and Justice.* Westview Press, 1992.

Colomeda, Lori. *Keepers of the Central Fire: Issues of Health and Ecology for Indigenous People.* National League of Nursing, 1998.

Davis, Shelton H. *Indigenous Views of Land and the Environment.* World Bank Discussion Papers, 188. 1993.

Dennee, JoAnne. *In the Three Sisters' Garden.* Food Works, 1995.

Dower, Roger C., et al., eds. *Frontiers of Sustainability: Environ-*

mentally Sound Agriculture, Forestry, Transportation, and Power Production. Island Press, 1997.

Dunmire, W.W. and G.D. Tierney. *Wild Plants of the Pueblo Province*. Museum of New Mexico Press, 1995.

Frankel, Carl. *In Earth's Company: Business, Environment, and the Challenge of Sustainability*. New Society Publishers, 1998.

Freeman, Milton M.R., ed. *Inuit, Whaling, and Sustainability*. Altamira Press, 1998.

Gedicks, Al and Winona LaDuke. *The New Resource Wars: Native and Environmental Struggles Against Multinational Corporations*. South End Press, 1993.

Grinde, Donald A. Jr., et al., eds. *Ecocide of Native America: Environmental Destruction of Indian Lands and Peoples*. Clear Light, 1998.

Hawken, Paul. *The Ecology of Commerce: A Declaration of Sustainability*. HarperBusiness, 1994.

InterCommission Task Forces on Indigenous Peoples. *Indigenous Peoples and Sustainability: Cases and Actions*. International Book Center of Atlanta, 1998.

Johnson, Huey D. and David R. Bower. *Green Plans: Greenprint for Sustainability*. University of Nebraska Press, 1997.

Kavasch, Barrie E. *Enduring Harvests: Native American Foods and Festivals for Every Season*. The Globe Pequot Press, 1995.

Kaya, Yoichi, et al., eds. *Environment, Energy, and Economy: Strategies for Sustainability*. Brookings Institution, 1998.

Lewis, David Rich. *Neither Wolf Nor Dog: American Indians, Environment, and Agrarian Change*. Oxford University Press, 1997.

Moore, Michael. *Medicinal Plants of the Mountain West*. Museum of New Mexico Press, 1979.

Orr, David. W. *Earth in Mind: On Education, Environment and the Human Prospect*. Island Press, 1994.

Peet, John. *Energy and the Ecological Economics of Sustainability.* Island Press, 1992.

Pitchford, Paul. *Healing with Whole Foods: Oriental Traditions and Modern Nutrition.* North Atlantic Books, 1993.

Pretty, Jules N. *Regenerating Agriculture: Policies and Practice for Sustainability and Self-Reliance.* National Academy Press, 1995.

Rogers, John J.W. and P. Geoffrey Feiss. *People and the Earth: Basic Issues in the Sustainability of Resources and Environment.* Cambridge University Press, 1998.

Samples, Bob. *Open Mind-Whole Mind: Parenting and Teaching Tomorrow's Children Today.* Jalmar Press, 1987.

Sandberg, L. Anders and Sverker Sorlin, eds. *Sustainability—The Challenge: People, Power, and the Environment.* Black Rose Books, 1999.

Smith, Joseph Wayne, et al. *The Bankruptcy of Economics: Ecology, Economics and the Sustainability of the Earth.* St. Martin's Press, 1998.

Weaver, Jace and Russell Means, eds. *Defending Mother Earth: Native American Perspectives on Environmental Justice.* Orbis Books, 1996.

Weil, Andrew. *Health and Healing.* Houghton Mifflin, 1983.

Index